CHOCOLATE
An Illustrated History

CHOCOLATE
An Illustrated History

MARCIA and FREDERIC MORTON

CROWN PUBLISHERS, INC.

New York

For Rebecca
with chocolate love and kisses

Published by Crown Publishers, Inc., 225 Park Avenue South, New York, New York 10003
Manufactured in Japan
CROWN is a trademark of Crown Publishers, Inc.

Library of Congress Cataloging in Publication Data

Morton, Frederic.
Chocolate, an illustrated history.

Includes index.
1. Chocolate—History.   2. Chocolate candy—History.
3. Chocolate industry—History.   I. Morton, Marcia.
II. Title.
TX817.C4M67
1986   641.3′374   85–15194
ISBN 0-517-55765-7

Design by Rhea Braunstein

10 9 8 7 6 5 4 3 2 1
First Edition

Contents

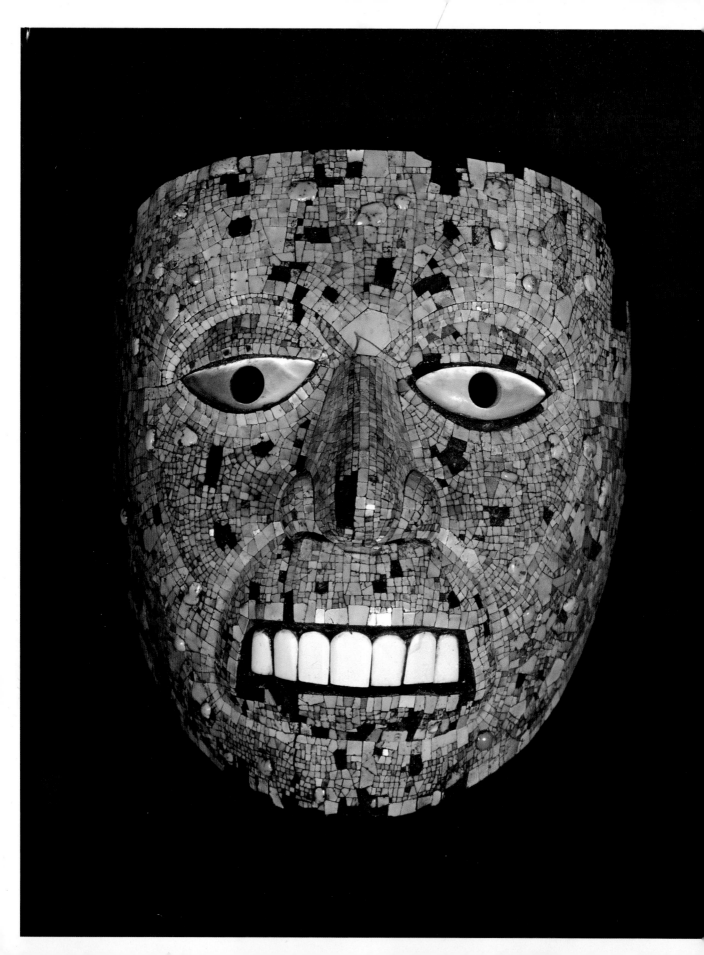

1

Montezuma's Golden Goblet of Xocoatl

*C*hocolate is divine, we all know that—divine as in delicious, delectable . . . a-a-ahhh. But chocolate really is *divine—divine as in heaven-born*. It came on this earth as the gift of a god. And earthly incarnations of divinity—emperors, kings, princesses—have always made it their own before passing it down to the rest of humanity. Today it still suggests luxury, opulence, and pleasure. Whether it comes as a forty-five-cent bar or a thirty-dollar boxful of gilt-

Aztec turquoise mosaic mask of Quetzalcoatl, the god worshipped by the Aztecs as the giver of chocolate to the world. *The British Museum—Museum of Mankind*

Early French engraving shows Aztec ("*Americain*") with his chocolate pot (*right foreground*) and goblet (*left*). The lower section of the picture shows a branch of the cocoa tree above a bundle of vanilla beans, which are also Central American natives and have been used as a flavoring for chocolate since Aztec times.

wrapped sculpted *fantaisies,* chocolate is always the special thing.

It is to food what mink is to clothing: not a basic necessity, but infinitely and almost universally desirable. Of course, there are those who don't like chocolate—there are those who don't like soft, warm mink—and this book is not for them, any more than is a chocolate truffle melting sumptuously on the tongue. But for everyone else, the ultimate product of the cocoa tree has been irresistible in every culture it has blessed.

Cocoa trees have grown, wild at first, in Central America for over four thousand years. Beautiful and bright-leafed, they bring forth pods filled with beans that are processed into chocolate. But before people discovered the wonderful treat nestling inside those bean pods, birds and monkeys lit on cocoa trees, tasted their fruit, and became the world's first chocophiles. In the course of their blithe nibbling they spread cocoa seeds around Central America—good little creatures, preparing a bountiful feast for humans.

Bountiful but not edible, not until the nineteenth century. For a long time no human being thought of chocolate as anything but a beverage. Ancient Central American tribes drank chocolate—and the Toltecs thought so much of it that when they burned incense before the altars of their gods, each worshipper was given a cocoa branch as a religious token. The rites culminated in the sacrifice of chocolate-colored dogs. And talk about sacrifice! To propitiate *their* chocolate god, the men of pre-Columbian Nicaragua offered up their sex lives. They lived celibate for thirteen days before venturing to sow the seed for new cocoa trees, in the hope of thus persuading the moon god to protect the crop. The same hope led the Itzá of Mexico to sacrifice a prisoner to their goddesses of food and water, after first sanctifying him by giving him a cup of chocolate to drink. Then the victim's heart, turned into a cocoa pod by the drink, would be torn from his body as a sacrificial offering.

When it came to human sacrifice, the Aztecs of Mexico outdid all others, tearing out men's hearts by the thousands—all in the name of glory to their principal deity, the sun god Huitzilopochtli, their champion in war. But the Aztecs had another god, almost as important to them, who was a benevolent figure personifying wisdom and knowledge—and it was he who gave them chocolate. His name was Quetzalcoatl, he was bearded and white-skinned, and he came from the Land of Gold where the sun rests at night. In the time before memory he was born of a god and a virgin mortal, endowed with all knowledge and wisdom. He had come down to Mexico to be the people's priest-king and to teach them the arts: painting and the working of silver, wood, and feathers. He had given the Aztecs their calendar, shown them how to grow maize. And from heaven he had brought the seeds of the cocoa tree. He showed his people how to grow the tree and how to make chocolate from it.

Quetzalcoatl's soul was so pure that his whole realm was happy and prosperous as long as he ruled. But he grew old. He thought his ugliness must terrify the people, and he decided to leave them, though to do so filled him with sadness. He burned his palace with its apartments of gold, jade, turquoise, bloodstone, pearls, and precious shells. He buried his treasures in the Mexican mountains, transformed his cocoa trees into mesquite, and departed as his multicolored birds flew ahead. (Today a certain rare, gorgeous Central American parrot is named the quetzal.) He wandered until he came to the place where sky, land, and water meet. From there he sailed away on a raft of serpents, back to the Land of Gold, where he still rules. Before he left, he promised to return—in the year "One Reed," which occurred once in every cycle of fifty-two years on the calendar Quetzalcoatl had created for the Aztecs.

Meantime, the cocoa seeds brought to earth by a god were spread by monkeys, birds, and man. Especially man. The Toltecs, the Itzá, and also the Maya knew cocoa. It was the Maya who first planted the seeds in Yucatán, when they expanded from their original home in Guatemala. About A.D. 600 they established in Yucatán history's first cocoa plantations. These, plus the plantations they developed elsewhere in their lands, brought great wealth to the Maya, who were important traders in Central America. Cocoa trees were considered so val-

Aztec stone figure of a man holding a cocoa pod, from between 1440 and 1521. *The Brooklyn Museum: Museum Collection Fund*

Benzoni's *History of the New World* depicted Aztecs roasting cocoa beans over a fire (*left*), crushing them to a paste (*right*), and pouring the *xocoatl* beverage (*rear*).

uable that their beans were used as currency throughout the region. Purchases were priced by the bean: eight for a rabbit, one hundred for a slave. Mexican picture script used a basketful of eight thousand cocoa beans to show the figure 8,000. And when the Aztecs defeated rival tribes, such as the Maya, sacks of cocoa beans were among the tribute they exacted.

Christopher Columbus was the first European to come upon this chocolate-flavored society. On his fourth voyage to the New World, in 1502, he tasted cocoa in Nicaragua, but was not impressed. His lack of response can be explained, perhaps, by his fixation on other flavors—the spices of India—and his dream of finding sea routes to them. Or maybe he just wasn't introduced properly to the strange new drink. It remained for another Spanish explorer, Hernán Cortés, to meet chocolate in an atmosphere fabulous enough to quicken all his perceptions.

In 1519 the Aztecs, under Emperor Montezuma II, were at the zenith of their brilliant civilization in Mexico, raised high above the simple folk who had offered chocolate to Columbus. Montezuma was "a gastronomic artist," as a French writer would later call him. His banquets were lavish feasts, imperially served: venison and other game, all manner of dainty birds, and exotic fruits. After the food was cleared away, entertainers would sing and dance and amuse the diners. Then, as the grand finale, servingwomen would perform a ceremonial washing of their hands and bring the honored guests *xocoatl*—chocolate—cold and frothy, mixed with honey, spices, and vanilla (another Central

Hernán Cortés, the Conquistador. He was the first to bring chocolate to Europe.

American native), and served at Montezuma's court in a kind of cup made of gold or gold-chased polished tortoiseshell. That was how Cortés first tasted chocolate. No wonder he was impressed.

That year, 1519, happened to coincide with "One Reed" on the Aztec calendar—the year that Quetzalcoatl had marked for his return. The Aztecs waited, as they had waited every fifty-two years, in hopes that this was the prophesied "One Reed" at last. When Cortés and his troops appeared, white-skinned and bearded as in the ancient chronicles, and marched on the Aztec capital of Tenochtitlán, they seemed to be the living fulfillment of Quetzalcoatl's promise. He had come back! The people rejoiced, and the emperor welcomed the god with a great banquet topped off with goblets of *xocoatl.*

Disillusion must have set in fast when the presumed Quetzalcoatl—he who had given his people chocolate—seemed not to have drunk it before, nor even to like it. Of course, *xocoatl* (*chocolatl,* it was pronounced) was not the luscious "chocolate" that would evolve. Pure chocolate straight from the bean, untamed by sugar, is a powerfully bitter shock to the palate at best. And early cocoa beans were harsher than the ones that scientific agriculture would later develop. The Central American tribes used their beans to make what were, by all accounts, rather bitter, peppery drinks, like the one served to Cortés.

If the taste didn't thrill him, the mystique surrounding the strange beverage did. The Aztecs thought it was intoxicating, and perhaps those strong early beans were, a bit. (Even today's chocolate is, if not intoxicating, just a little stimulating by virtue of its slight caffeine content.) Besides, the Aztecs often mixed chocolate with wine instead of water, or with fermented corn mash, and they drank so much of such brews that they might indeed have ended up more or less high. They put pimiento and pepper into their chocolate. Sometimes they even added the ground bones of ancestors and took the concoction as medicine for dysentery.

Montezuma apparently drank his chocolate merely honeyed and spiced. But it was all he drank, at the rate of fifty flagons a day, not counting the golden goblet of *xocoatl* he downed each time he prepared to enter his harem. For part of chocolate's mystique was a firm belief in its aphrodisiac powers. In addition, the drink was supposed to give mere mortals a portion of Quetzalcoatl's wisdom. Finally—and probably of most importance to the war-minded, empire-building Aztecs—chocolate was so certain to confer vigor and strength that in early times it was reserved for rulers and soldiers.

In Montezuma's imperial household everyone drank it: two thousand pitcherfuls a day, though not all from the golden goblets Montezuma used. Each time the emperor drained one of these, he tossed it into the lake outside his palace. Years later, when the Aztec empire was long gone, divers were still bringing up golden relics from their watery trove. Like another emperor in another time and place—Nero in ancient Rome—Montezuma sent runners to scoop up fresh mountain snow for his delectation. But the Romans had only flavored syrups to trickle over their snow. Montezuma poured out *xocoatl* and refreshed himself with the first chocolate ice.

The luxury and the mystique impressed Cortés. "The divine drink," he called chocolate in a letter to his king, Charles I of Spain, "which builds up resistance and fights fatigue. A cup of this precious drink permits a man to walk for a whole day without food." It was an assessment of chocolate that would continue in Europe for centuries. Cortés assessed something else: the use of cocoa beans as currency. He established a cocoa plantation of his own—or rather of Charles V's own—to thus grow money for the Spanish treasury. And he took beans with him to plant when he sailed to Haiti, Trinidad, and Fernando Po, an island off Africa's west coast.

But first he pursued his conquering marches through Mexico. Hernán Cortés was not the second coming of Quetzalcoatl, the benevolent god. He was the Conquistador, and he brought the Aztecs, not wisdom and arts, but the destruction of their civilization and the debasement of their empire to a Spanish colony. Heinrich Heine, the liberal-minded nineteenth-century German poet, wrote an angry verse about it:

> *Only a robber captain was he,*
> *Who in the book of fate inscribed*
> *With his own insolent fist*
> *His insolent name: Cortés!*

Old *Harper's New Monthly Magazine* illustration of Cortés's meeting with a delegation sent by Montezuma to welcome him. The Aztec woman beside Cortés is probably Malintzin, the historical basis for his interpreter/mistress as portrayed in Donald Barthelme's story.

The year after Montezuma welcomed Cortés to Mexico with a banquet fit for a god, Cortés responded with a treachery that has echoed through the ages. He arrested the pagan emperor and claimed his lands for a Christian monarch. Almost half a millennium later the acclaimed postmodernist American author Donald Barthelme fictionalized the event in a story called "Cortés and Montezuma." In it, Cortés is asleep beside his Aztec mistress "in the palace given him by Montezuma. Cortés awakens; they share a cup of chocolate." Cortés goes off to meet Montezuma. They become friends, and the story consists largely of their intellectual exchanges on politics and religion. In the end Cortés arrests Montezuma, "in the kindest possible way," and tells him, not entirely sanctimoniously, "Our Lord Jesus Christ loves you." To which Barthelme has Montezuma reply, deadpan, "I'll send Him chocolate."

In historical fact, Cortés had Montezuma imprisoned in irons. When the Aztecs rebelled at the desecration, Cortés ordered the emperor to calm them from the prison walls. As Montezuma spoke, his frenzied subjects hurled arrows and stones at their humbled emperor, and he was killed—either by one of the stones or by the Spanish, secretly; the truth was never made clear. Montezuma the grandiloquent died, shackled, in ignominy. His most enduring bequest to world culture was chocolate.

A year after his murder, his successor was executed by Cortés's troops. Two years later, in 1523, a royal governor arrived from Madrid, the first in a line that would rule Mexico as a Spanish possession for three hundred years.

2

The Divine Drink Captivates Europe

*I*n 1528, his mission of conquest accomplished, Cortés sailed home to Spain with a boatload of gifts from the New World. Not the least of them were cocoa beans, plus the techniques Cortés had learned for harvesting the tree—named cacao *by the* Spanish, from the Aztec cacahuatl—*to brewing the final* elixir—chocolate *in Spanish, from the Mayan/Aztec* xocoatl. *Cortés had seen how the pods were picked from the cocoa trees; how the beans inside were removed, then spread out in the sun to ferment and dry; and, finally,*

"La Xocolatada," Catalonian panel from about 1720, made out of glazed earthenware tiles. The gentlemen are serving hot chocolate to the ladies, and (*lower right*) are preparing it from the little rods of chocolate on the ground.

Frontispiece of a 1639 book about chocolate, written in Latin. Neptune is being handed a casket of chocolate to carry across the sea to Europe.

Plate from Dufour's *Treatises on Coffee, Tea, and Chocolate* (1688) acknowledges Europe's debt to the Arabs, the Chinese, and the Aztecs—respectively—for the three beverages, and shows the characteristic serving vessel for each. A *molinet* lies beside the chocolate pot.

how the dried beans were roasted over a fire, then crushed in a stone trough, between stone rollers, to an aromatic paste which was mixed with water to make a beverage. Cortés even took along the Aztec utensils used to prepare chocolate, to let the Spanish emperor taste it.

Charles V was fascinated by the new flavor, but he thought it could use a little sugar. Luckily, cane sugar was already known in Europe, being imported from the Orient. It was still very expensive, but so was chocolate, which had to be brought from an equally far-off country. The two flavors were natural partners, making a rare and costly drink that the royals and nobles of the Spanish court simply adored. Sometimes the cocoa paste was mixed with honey and spices, *à la* Montezuma, instead of sugar; sometimes with orange or rose water, or cinnamon, vanilla, almonds, pistachios, musk, nutmeg, cloves, allspice, aniseed. Always the drink was served cold, thick enough to hold up a spoon, and swizzled to a froth with a utensil adopted from the Aztecs—a wooden stick with several concentric, loose disks at one end. The Spanish christened it a *molinet*, probably from the verb *moler*, "to beat"; it is used in Latin America to this day. When some Spaniard came up with the refinement of serving chocolate hot and pouring it from a pot, the *molinet* was retained. A chocolate pot differed little from a coffeepot, except that usually there was a small hole in the lid through which to fit the swizzle stick.

The chocolate itself, during those early days in Spain, was prepared by monks in their cloisters. It was a hallowed tradition. Monastery kitchens had long served as workshops for the creation of delicious new recipes. Now they perfected the roasting and grinding of cocoa beans, the shaping of chocolate into

Diorama based on a seventeenth-century engraving of Spanish monks conferring over their hot chocolate. *Chocolate Manufacturers Association of U.S.A.*

little rods or tablets to be dissolved as required in aristocratic salons. (Freshly made chocolate is a paste, almost liquid from the friction-generated heat of the grinding. It is easily shaped and hardens quickly at room temperature.) The good brothers themselves grew fond of a cup of the fragrant, steaming brew.

All the Spanish who could afford it were mad for chocolate. It began to be mentioned in story and song. "When will the day come," went an Andalusian love ballad, "that blissful morning when chocolate will be brought to both of us in bed?" Throughout the sixteenth century the Spanish kept their rhapsodizing to themselves, unwilling to share with other countries the precious cocoa beans that had to be brought from Mexico with much effort. By the end of the century regular shipments were coming across the ocean from the increasing number of Spanish-Mexican cocoa plantations. In the Atlantic marauding battles of the time, when a Spanish frigate was captured by Dutch or

English ships, the boarding sailors would scavenge everything of value but toss into the sea the nameless, meaningless cocoa beans they found. They had no idea that those "worthless" beans were a highly taxed luxury item in Spain.

But little by little, word of the new drink began to trickle out. In the early 1600s the Spanish court was Europe's trend-setter in things fashionable. Travelers came to Madrid to sample its elegancies, among them the sipping of chocolate. An Italian named Antonio Carletti took the custom home with him, and Italy embarked on its long, inventive way with chocolate. Spanish monks offered a taste to visiting brothers from abroad. Foreign sailors, hearing tales of all this, stopped dumping cocoa beans overboard and realized that it made more sense to smuggle them into their own countries instead.

Still Life: Limes, Box of Sweets, and Other Objects by Luis Meléndez. One of the other objects is a *jícara*—a special Spanish word reserved for a cup (this one was brought from Mexico) in which to drink chocolate. *Derechos Reservados © Museo del Prado, Madrid*

Still Life: Chocolate Service by Luis Meléndez, eighteenth-century Spanish. The pot has a *molinet;* chocolate tablets (*lower right*) were dissolved in hot water to make the drink. *Derechos Reservados © Museo del Prado, Madrid*

Two eighteenth-century Spanish-Mexican chocolate goblets, made of coconut shells mounted in silver. *I.N.A.H., Mexico*

Back in its birthplace, Mexico, the Spanish had succeeded by now in establishing a large colonial society. On the ashes, still warm, of Montezuma's capital of Tenochtitlán they had erected New Spain's new capital, Mexico City. On the stones of the Aztec sun god's temple they had built the Catholic cathedral. Other churches filled the colony, and in them the Spanish-Mexican ladies got into the habit of having chocolate served during mass, fortifying the flesh while nourishing the spirit. Their bishop censured such unbecoming frivolity. Soon afterward someone—the affronted *doñas* had no idea who—slipped poison into the bishop's morning cup of chocolate. His death conjured uncanny echoes of the ancient Mexican Itzá tribe, which had prepared victims for sacrifice by giving them chocolate to drink.

People were beginning to write about chocolate. In 1609 the first book on the subject was published, appropriately in Mexico: *Libro en el cual se trata del chocolate* (*Book Treating of Chocolate*). In 1648 the Englishman Thomas Gage reported in *A New Survey of the West Indies* that "all, rich or poor, loved to drink plain chocolate without sugar or other ingredients." The Spanish had planted cocoa as they conquered around the Caribbean, so that chocolate was indeed drunk by all, rich or poor. In Colombia, from fifteenth-century colonial days to the present, the afternoon chocolate break has been a national pastime. In Jamaica, which the Spanish ruled until the English wrested it away in 1655, the black plantation slaves drank it "for the better support of nature in their hard labor." Thomas Gage adopted the habit himself, to the tune of five cups a day for twelve years, thereby attaining excellent health, he assured his readers. For-

Anne of Austria, the Spanish princess who introduced chocolate into France when she married Louis XIII.

Louis XIII

tunately, by then the English, thus tantalized by Gage, did not have long to wait for their own introduction to chocolate.

Already in 1615 the Spanish had realized the hopelessness of trying to keep their secret any longer. That year they'd decided to go public with a royal splash. The occasion was the marriage of the infanta, Anne of Austria to the king next door, Louis XIII of France. (Anne of Austria was the Spanish princess, her misleading title notwithstanding. She inherited the title as the eldest child of Philip III, king of Spain, but by birth a Habsburg from the imperial house of Austria.) The fourteen-year-old bride took along the glamorous gift of Spanish chocolate for her fourteen-year-old betrothed.

Nonetheless, the marriage was neither happy nor, for a long time, fruitful. Young Louis didn't trouble to hide his distaste for females generally, and his girl wife in particular. He hardly touched her. It took the couple twenty-three years to grow up and produce an heir. But when Anne finally did get pregnant she brought forth a wonder: the Sun King, Louis XIV, who would outdo Montezuma himself in the splendor of his reign at Versailles.

Chocolate had a faster time of it than Anne did in their new country. The French court took up the queen's gift enthusiastically. Louis XIII's great mentor Cardinal Richelieu, for one, credited chocolate drinking for his vigorous activity, in the course of which he won for his monarch the absolute power that would descend to Anne's son. Richelieu's brother gained his own benefits from chocolate. He used it "to modify the vapors of his spleen and to fight against fits of anger and bad moods." Chocolate could do anything, it seemed. To the courtiers it was a symbol of chic. After Louis XIII died in 1643, Anne governed France as regent for eight years, until her son was old enough to take the throne; one of the most sought-after invitations in Paris was "to the chocolate of her Royal Highness." For court belles and beaux chocolate was part of *l'amour,* as in a popular story going around about a noblewoman who, betrayed by her lover, revenged herself by pouring him a poisoned cup. He drank it, the

Maria Theresa, Spanish consort of Louis XIV, had two passions: the king and chocolate.

Louis XIV

story went, with Gallic insouciance, saying only, "The chocolate would have been better, my dear, if you had added a little more sugar—the poison gives it a bitter flavor. Think of this the next time you offer a gentleman chocolate." And he fell gallantly dead at her feet.

For one Parisian shopkeeper chocolate meant an opportunity to go into business abroad. In 1657 he crossed the Channel and opened London's first chocolate shop. "An excellent West India drink called chocolate" was announced in the *Publick Advertiser* that June. "In Bishopsgate Street, in Queen's Head Alley, at a Frenchman's house . . . ready at any time, and also unmade at reasonable rates." The English could finally unbate the breath they'd been holding ever since Thomas Gage had set them agog a decade earlier.

Meantime, back in Paris, Louis XIV had ascended the throne and was of an age to marry. Anne had the perfect bride for her son: a new Spanish princess, Maria Theresa, daughter of the new Spanish king, Philip IV, Anne's brother. In 1660 the two young cousins were married. Once again a Spanish royal bride came to France with a betrothal gift of chocolate, an ornate box filled with it. This second Iberian infusion solidified chocolate's dominion in France for good and all. Maria Theresa was a devoted consort, of whom the court quipped that she had two passions, the king and chocolate. Accordingly, in his newlywed glow Louis appointed a Paris merchant as court purveyor of "a certain composition which is named chocolate."

Louis XIV, unlike his father, did like women, a lot. He also greatly loved his strict Spanish mother. While she lived, during the first six years of his marriage, he hid his dalliances out of respect for her propriety. After that, *le déluge.* And chocolate, which had come to France twice as a conjugal offering, now skipped to the extramarital. For instance, Madame de Maintenon, as Louis's mistress until he finally made her his morganatic wife after Maria Theresa died, took on his chocolate drinking along with the Sun King.

Spain had been more generous than it knew when it sent its princesses out into the world bearing gifts of chocolate. Apparently, to taste the stuff was to crave it. Every country that learned about chocolate started looking for its own source of supply. Spain pretty much had the trade sewn up through the seventeenth century. Spanish colonizers started cocoa plantations wherever the climate was right—Venezuela, the Philippines . . . (cocoa trees thrive at latitudes between twenty degrees south and twenty degrees north of the equator)—and Spanish prices and taxes were high, their shipments of cocoa beans limited. Other countries, with their own New World territories, decided to share the profits and at the same time provide for their own chocolate craving.

In 1660, the very year Louis XIV's bride completed chocolate's conquest of France, the French looked to their future by starting cocoa cultivation on their West Indies island of Martinique. Further, for a century and a half France had been running raids into Brazil, trying to undermine Portugal's control of that vast country. In 1677 the French used chocolate for the job, establishing cocoa plantations as a kind of homesteading claim—and as a way of providing themselves with a good supply of their aristocracy's favorite beverage. The pattern would accelerate through the centuries as world demand grew.

The Cup of Chocolate by Jean-Baptiste Charpentier, eighteenth-century French. Pictured is the family of the Duke de Penthièvre—members of the French royal court, and thus of course devotees of the royal drink. *Cliché des Musées Nationaux, Paris*

3

London's Chocolate Houses

*A*lready *in 1662 upper-class French and Italians, not to speak of the Spanish, were consuming so much chocolate that their Catholic devotions seemed to be compromised. To wit: Was the drink too voluptuous an indulgence for the Lenten season? Cardinal Brancaccio of Rome examined the dilemma and pronounced in Latin, "Liquidum non frangit jejunum" ("Liquids [and therefore cups of chocolate] do not break the fast").*

Shriven, chocolate lovers could enjoy the potion in peace,

Mademoiselle de Charolais by Jean-Baptiste Pater, early-eighteenth-century French. Portrait of Louise-Anne de Bourbon-Condé. A cup of chocolate stands before the young noblewoman. She is wearing a "fantasy" monk's habit to show her devotion to the Franciscan order, and is knotting the waist cord to symbolize St. Francis of Assisi's three holy vows: poverty, chastity, obedience. Upper-class French Catholics, like those in Spain and Italy, worried that their fondness for drinking chocolate might imperil their observance of Lent. A cardinal in Rome reassured them. *Cliché des Musées Nationaux, Paris*

Engraving of a chocolate house. The beverage took on a raffish note in London, where it was introduced by a shopkeeper instead of a princess. *The Cocoa, Chocolate and Confectionery Alliance, London*

reassured that not only did it leave their souls intact, but it positively nurtured their bodies. A French medical student named Foucault wrote a thesis, *On the Healthful Uses of Chocolate,* while the famous Dr. Bachot gave his approval with "this beverage, well made, is such a noble confection that it is, more than nectar and ambrosia, the true food of the gods." In England another renowned physician, Henry Stubbe, also used the word *nectar*—"Indian nectar" was his phrase—but on the whole he was more coolly scientific. He contented himself with advising that one ounce of chocolate was loaded with more fat and nourishment than a pound of meat, and worked out precise chocolate blends to be taken as medicine. The year was 1662.

Samuel Pepys, the unflagging diarist of London in the 1660s, drank chocolate for the first time on a morning in 1662 "to settle my stomach." Evidently he liked it. In his diaries, where he scrupulously noted everything he ate and drank, from time to time he mentioned his "morning draft" of chocolate. In 1664, for instance, he breakfasted with a business colleague, "and there drank my morning draft in good chocollatte, and"—in his eagerness?—"slabbering my band [neckband] sent home for another."

Pepys did his share of wenching, and he may have been aware of Dr. Stubbe's further judgment, that chocolate "becomes provocative to lust upon no other account than that it begets good blood." Or of James Wadsworth's jolly quatrain in *A Curious History of the Nature and Quality of Chocolate:*

'Twill make Old women Young and Fresh;
Create New Motions of the Flesh,
And cause them long for you know what,
If they but taste of chocolate.

No doubt about it: chocolate, so fraught with chic at the royal courts in Madrid and Paris, took on a distinctly raffish note in London. It could well have had something to do with the way chocolate was introduced to England—not in exclusivity behind palace walls, but on sale in a shop. It was an apt provenance for what Adam Smith called this "nation of shopkeepers." In any case, chocolate was a relatively democratic, public item in London from the first.

Toward the end of the century, chocolate houses began to spring up, rivaling the coffeehouses the city had known since about 1650. The two kinds of establishment had much in common. Both offered food as well as their special beverages; often card playing, dice, and other gambling; and talk, always talk, talk about everything from poetry to gossip, politics to business.

Chocolate houses were central to London's gregarious—all-male gregarious—social life of the time. The patron, entering, would toss a penny on the counter to pay for admission to the place and the right to riffle through the free newssheets. Then he would pay for his chocolate, which wasn't cheap (the English government, like the Spanish, found it a lucrative tax item), and join a table of cronies to sip and chat.

Many of the patrons were the dashing, sporty young gentlemen called "bloods" in the era's slang. Their normal dinnertime was at three or four in the afternoon; by six they'd be carousing and gambling in the chocolate houses around Covent Garden or St. James's Street. Not surprisingly, things sometimes got too energetic. One night at the Royal Chocolate House, hangout for a wild band of bloods, a gambling dispute exploded into swordplay and three of the chaps were cut down. In the midst of it all one Colonel Cunningham sat blinking, fortunately with his devoted footman standing by. The stout fellow carried his colonel bodily through the whooshing swords and out of the room, uncut and undaunted. The Royal Guards were called in. When their pleas and threats didn't quiet the free-for-all, they swung their musket butts, knocking down bloods right and left. Quetzalcoatl, in the Land of Gold, must have looked down in horror at the brawl into which his *xocoatl* had fallen among the unruly British.

As a matter of fact, though the Aztecs did think *xocoatl* was intoxicating, it seems unlikely that the bloods were inflamed by mere chocolate. Probably their drink was made, not of sugar and spice, but of wine and other spirits diluting the chocolate; it was the seventeenth-century Englishman's mode. But not all chocolate houses were so rowdy. Some of the more aristocratic ones in the West End even banished smoking from their premises. And two—White's and the Cocoa Tree—attained real eminence.

Modern representation of aristocrats enjoying chocolate in an eighteenth-century English mansion—a less ebullient ambience than the chocolate houses. *Courtesy, Rowntree Mackintosh*

White's opened in 1697 as a chocolate house like any other, with gambling and the rest, run by Francis White. By 1709 the place stood out enough that when Richard Steele began to publish his boulevard newspaper *The Tatler* that year, in the first issue he promised that "all acounts of gallantry, pleasure, and entertainment shall be under the article of White's Chocolate House." Many of the paper's early issues were datelined White's, where Steele wrote them.

When Francis White died in 1711, his widow took over and lifted the place up the social ladder. Soon all London was talking about the fashionable society to be met there. The lady rose, too, being known first as the "Widow White," then "Mrs. White," and finally "Madam White." She was so confident of her house's appeal that she raised the admission price from the usual penny, and even more of the gilded set glided through her doors. White's trendiness was certified by newspaper ads for London's glossiest amusements, which listed "Mrs. White's Chocolate House, in St. James's Street" as the place to buy tickets—for opera performances at the Haymarket theater, for instance. When the London producer of Handel's operas switched his line of work, he remembered that. He was an emigrant Swiss named John James Heidegger, and he quickly became the talk of the town as the aristocracy's professional master of

A watercolor by Thomas Rowlandson, eighteenth-century English, showing a 1787 chocolate house, where the fashionable right people could do the wrong things. *The Museum of London*

the revels, a sort of early Elsa Maxwell. To make sure that admission cards to his balls, ridottos, and masquerades got only into the right hands, he issued them at White's. Those who didn't plan to attend were requested kindly to turn in their cards at White's as well, lest the wrong people get hold of them and crash his carefully cast galas.

Snobbish didn't mean stuffy, of course. It was perfectly fine for the right people to do the wrong things, so long as they did them stylishly. Gambling at White's, for example. In 1733 the place was still so well known for high-toned high stakes that the painter William Hogarth utilized it as a ready-made metaphor. In *A Rake's Progress,* his morality-play series of eight satiric engravings depicting the joys and dissipations of a blood, he set the gambling sequence in White's.

The other famous chocolate house, the Cocoa Tree, was never as fashionable as White's. But it had its own kind of distinction. It, too, attracted the patron-

Before the midcentury White's Chocolate House had changed its character and its address, becoming a private club in this dignified building.

age of Richard Steele (with his collaborator, Joseph Addison). And here, too, the writers turned out essays—for *The Tatler*'s successor, *The Spectator,* which began to appear in 1711. In a 1712 issue Addison wrote (tongue in cheek over his Cocoa Tree chocolate, one presumes): "I shall also advise my fair readers to be in a particular manner careful how they meddle with romances, chocolate, novels, and the like inflamers, which I look upon as very dangerous to be made use of." A winking reference, perhaps, to James Wadsworth's bawdy quatrain.

Coffeehouses and chocolate houses often drew specialized groups of customers: poets at one, politicians at another. The Cocoa Tree came down on the political side, soon being spoken of as "the Tory chocolate house. . . . A Whig will no more go to the Cocoa Tree . . . than a Tory will be seen at the coffee house of St. James's." By 1746 the Cocoa Tree had developed into the quasi-official headquarters of the Jacobite party in Parliament.

By then, though, the Cocoa Tree, like White's and a great many other leading chocolate houses and coffeehouses, had changed. They had been rather like informal clubs from the start, with congenial patrons who met regularly at

their tables. Before the midcentury, one by one the best houses found it profitable to reorganize as private clubs, with revenue coming in from affluent members rather than the unpredictable general public. London clubs, the city's male social bastion in the next centuries, rose in good part from a solid foundation of chocolate.

Gaming-house scene from *The Rake's Progress* by William Hogarth, eighteenth-century English. Hogarth set the scene in White's Chocolate House, which he used as a ready-made metaphor.

4

Floating on a *Theobroma* Cloud, from Europe to America

Chocolate houses—not always as colorful as those in London—were all over Europe. In a Belgian one in 1697 the visiting mayor of Zurich tasted his first sip. He took the tidings home to Switzerland (thus linking through chocolate two countries that would be preeminent in it nearly three centuries later). About the same time, chocolate appeared in Germany; as usual, the government soon put a heavy import duty on it. Also as usual, local medical men welcomed it with laudatory treatises. One of the greatest

The Cup of Chocolate by Nicolas Lancret, eighteenth-century French. The drink often figured in the era's depiction of elegance. *The National Gallery, London*

German scientists, Alexander von Humboldt, chimed in almost exactly a hundred years later. After spending several years in Central America, studying its botany among other things, he concluded, "The cocoa bean is a phenomenon, for nowhere else has nature concentrated such a wealth of valuable nourishment in so small a space."

During the intervening century, even before the Germans heard Humboldt's verdict, the popular drink was sold indoors and out until the emperor, Frederick the Great, clutched his ears in 1747 and prohibited street-hawking, specifically the cry of "Chocolate!" In Holland, though, an Amsterdam physician found a soothing effect. "Chocolate is not only pleasant of taste," he wrote, "but is also a veritable balm of the mouth, for the maintaining of all glands and humors in a good state of health. Thus it is, that all who do drink it, possess a sweet breath."

A citizen of Amsterdam had a right to feel proprietary about chocolate. For centuries the Netherlands had had a complicated involvement with Spain, mostly a matter of fighting off Spanish rule. In the course of Spain's intermittent dominion over their country, the Dutch had gotten a peek into the Spanish cocoa-bean secret before it went out into the rest of Europe. Amsterdam, one of Northern Europe's most important ports, sent its ships into the cocoa trade as early as the seventeenth century. The Dutch city became, and remains today, the world's largest cocoa port. From Holland would one day come a couple of inventions crucial to the development of modern chocolate. And from Belgium—which was part of the Netherlands during the long struggle with Spain—would come chocolate marvels.

In 1720 a Dutchman voyaged to the French island of Martinique, with its decades-old cocoa plantations. "There died recently in Martinique a Councillor of about a hundred years of age," the traveler reported. "He subsisted for thirty years on nothing other than chocolate and some biscuits. Occasionally he would take a little soup to eat, but at no time meat, fish, or other nourishment. Yet he was so fit that, at the age of eighty-five years, he could still mount his horse without stirrups."

Chocolate encouraged all sorts of physical prowess. The mighty lover Casanova found the drink as useful a lubricant to seduction as Champagne. He also liked to take a cup for breakfast, and mentioned the fact often in his memoirs. His fellow Italians were becoming famous for their superior chocolate. Masters from Venice and Florence journeyed throughout Europe to teach their skills.

Vienna got chocolate in 1711, by way of an intricate piece of royal politics. For a couple of hundred years Spain had been ruled by members of the house of Austria, the Habsburg dynasty; Anne of Austria and her niece Maria Theresia, the two princesses dowered with chocolate, were Spanish Habsburgs. In 1700 the line died out. To rejuvenate it, an Austrian Habsburg prince was proclaimed King Charles III of Spain, and for years he kept trying to enter Madrid and give his title substance. He had little success. When his elder brother died in 1711, leaving the Austrian throne vacant, Charles regretfully left Spain to

Emperor Charles VI in his coronation robes. The event bestowed the Austrian crown on him—and chocolate on Vienna.

become Austria's Emperor Charles VI instead. Among the happier souvenirs he took along to Vienna was chocolate.

As in other royal and imperial courts, the Viennese aristocracy quickly adopted the new drink. When Charles's daughter Maria Theresia succeeded him, everyone knew that her consort, Emperor Franz, simply had to have his cup every morning. So, naturally, all the courtiers did, too. Maria Theresia's court poet even wrote a "Cantata to Chocolate," and he began each day with . . . need one ask? By a little maneuvering, the influential managed to get hold of the sought-after Spanish chocolate through Austria's embassy in Madrid. They poured it frothing from pots with the *molinet* opening in the lid, drank it from Chinese porcelain cups set in silver holders, on tortoiseshell saucers. For the imperial couple, both holder and saucer were gold.

Austria's Empress Maria Theresia and her family at their morning chocolate. Aquarelle, about 1760, by an elder daughter, Archduchess Maria Christine, showing herself (*left*), her parents, and three of their fifteen other children. The little girl with the doll is five-year-old Marie Antoinette, future queen of France. *Kunsthistorische Museum, Vienna*

Since Austria didn't overload chocolate with taxes, it was affordable for people outside the aristocracy. A traveler from Berlin—where levies were prohibitive—told in his memoirs how shocked he'd been to see a Viennese *tailor* drinking chocolate, and top-grade chocolate at that. Vienna, he decided, was a den of sybarites!

In 1743 the fashionable Swiss painter Jean-Etienne Liotard was called to the Austrian capital on a commission to portray Empress Maria Theresia and her family. During his Viennese sojourn Liotard was awakened every morning by a chambermaid named Nandl Baldauf, bringing his breakfast chocolate. Nandl was pretty, and something in her charming little daily errand struck his artist's eye. He asked her to pose for him just as she appeared in his room each morning. The ensuing picture, *La Belle Chocolatière* (*The Beautiful Chocolate Girl*), became the most popular painting ever to deal with a chocolate theme. Nandl

Several of the thirty pieces in Maria Theresia's "great breakfast service." The shallow cup was used for tea; the taller, narrower one, mounted in gold, with a gold saucer, was for chocolate. Both cups are Chinese porcelain. The teapot (rear) and chocolate pot are gold vermeil. *Kunsthistorische Museum, Vienna*

went on to live a penny-novel romance. For twenty-five years she was the light o' love of a Viennese nobleman. In the end he married her and turned the Chocolate Girl chambermaid into Princess Dietrichstein. As for her picture, it became not only a museum work of art but the trademark for Baker's chocolate in America.

Another kind of immortality descended on chocolate in Sweden. In the mid-eighteenth century the great Swedish naturalist Linnaeus set about classifying all the flora then known to European botanists. He devised Greek and Latin names as he saw fit. About the cocoa tree he said, "The fruit supplies the raw product for a most delicious, healthy and nourishing drink." And he gave the cocoa its enduring Greek botanical name, with a bow to Quetzalcoatl. *Theobroma,* it is called to this day: "Food of the gods."

Europe floated on a chocolate cloud. Yet there weren't really that many cocoa beans coming over from the New World. Major global cultivation was at least a century away. In 1693 in chocophile France the largest cocoa merchant had only about ten pounds to sell, out of about twenty-two pounds in the whole country. (In 1983 France imported 55,000 tons of cocoa beans.) Still, the time had come to send chocolate back across the Atlantic—specifically, to the burgeoning British colonies that would become the U.S.A., home of the free, the brave, and, in its own dubious coinage, the chocoholic.

Most chocolate historians fix on 1755 as the year when *Theobroma* truly arrived in the colonies. The Dutch had brought in a little as early as New Amsterdam days, when old Amsterdam was already plying the cocoa trade. English colonists of the 1600s liked to take chocolate after hearty breakfasts of meat, fish, poultry, and vegetables. They flattered themselves that the drink helped a stomach called upon for such heroic efforts. And already in 1712 a Boston apothecary was advertising chocolate for sale. But 1755 is the epochal date, because that was when colonists went into the business for themselves. Massachusetts sea captains began sailing to the Caribbean to trade for cocoa beans directly, in their own hemisphere. At home ports like Salem and Marblehead, or Newport, Rhode Island, their cargoes sold for less than shipments from the mother country, which had to cross the Atlantic twice, from the West Indies to Europe, then back to North America. The customers were apothecaries. Chocolate had always beckoned to humanity with much more than flavor. Wisdom, vigor, sexuality, health . . . what couldn't chocolate give you? Especially, in the colonies, health. People drank chocolate as a medicine, what they called a "confection"; that is, a medicine coaxed into palatability by mixing it with pleasant tastes like sugar (though one physician in London had cautioned that chocolate, nutritious in itself, turned poisonous when combined with sugar). Since doctors and apothecaries were experienced at preparing "confec-

The Beautiful Chocolate Girl by Jean-Etienne Liotard (1743), Swiss. A pretty chambermaid brought the artist's breakfast drink and became his model for the world's most popular chocolate painting. *Gemäldegalerie, Alte Meister Staatliche Kunstsammlungen, Dresden*

tions" with mortar and pestle, they added chocolate to their arsenal and became its first colonial purveyors.

Logically enough, it was a physician who began what would one day be the giant chocolate industry of the United States. In 1765 Dr. James Baker of Dorchester, Massachusetts, joined forces with a chocolate maker newly arrived from Ireland, John Hannon. Dr. Baker put up the money to rent space in a gristmill at Milton Lower Mills on the Neponset River, and Hannon ground cocoa beans with the water power outside their door instead of the apothecaries' mortar and pestle. The first real chocolate factory in the Bay Colony—today the oldest chocolate company in the United States—was in operation. In 1777 they were advertising their product, which apparently was either sold for cash or ground from the customer's own cocoa beans. The ad ended with a promise that would become an American article of faith, the money-back guarantee:

Hannon's Best CHOCOLATE
Marked upon each cake J.H.N.
Warranted pure, and ground exceeding fine.
Where may be had any Quantity, from 50 wt. to
a ton, for Cash or Cocoa, at his Mills in Milton.
N.B. If the Chocolate does not prove good, the
Money will be returned.

In 1779 Hannon sailed for the West Indies to buy cocoa beans for the factory and was lost at sea. The business became the Baker Company; then, when Dr. James's grandson took over in 1820, it became the Walter Baker Company, notable to this day for its ubiquitous one-inch squares of baking chocolate, the basic building blocks for almost every brownie made in America.

Aside from Baker, there wasn't much company-size chocolate activity during the transition years when the colonies were transforming themselves into an independent republic. In 1786 the New York City directory showed only three chocolate makers; Philadelphia, seat of the fledgling government, had four. But Thomas Jefferson predicted, "The superiority of chocolate, both for health and nourishment, will soon give it the same preference over tea and coffee in America which it has in Spain."

Across the sea in London, the public's possible preference for chocolate over ale was at issue. Tavern keepers complained about the foreign drink's inroads on the traditional English tankard. In 1763 ale and beer interests had even pushed for legislation against the import of cocoa beans. They were unsuccessful. In fact, in 1776 the chocolate maker Joseph Fry submitted his own "Hum-

Breakfast by Jean-Etienne Liotard (1754). Another of Liotard's several paintings about chocolate drinking. *Sammlung der Bay. Hypoth. u. Wechselbank in der Alten Pinakothek, Munich. Photo by Joachim Blauel, ARTOTHEK*

Gilt vermeil chocolate pot, with its heater and sugar bowl, belonging to Marie Leszcynska, Louis XV's Polish-born queen. *Cliché des Musées Nationaux, Paris*

ble Memorial to the Lords Commissioners of the Treasury," petitioning them to lower the tax on chocolate. In time, that effort would succeed.

Over in *ancien régime* France chocolate tripped along with the Bourbon kings. After Louis XIII and XIV, Louis XV took the throne in 1723, at the age of thirteen. His two most famous mistresses during his fifty-year reign, *les mesdames* Du Barry and Pompadour, continued the royal chocolate connection. Du Barry was the object of much lascivious pamphleteering, a great deal of it untrue and unjust. Among the diatribes was the damning charge that she plied her lovers with chocolate to whip up their ardor in gratifying her lust. Her predecessor, Pompadour, had the opposite problem. In his biography of Du Barry, Stanley Loomis wrote:

> Pompadour's had been the paradox of some great concert pianist born with insufficient fingers, for this woman who is one of history's

Louis XV, whose two most celebrated paramours continued the royal French chocolate connection.

HILDIBRANY SC

ADeN

Madame de Pompadour by François Boucher. A king's mistress—but her passion was for the arts rather than for passion, and she drank chocolate to make up the difference. *National Galleries of Scotland, Edinburgh*

most celebrated courtesans was, in fact, frigid. To warm a temperament that was by nature cool, to stir a sensuality that was at best sluggish, she had recourse to curious aphrodisiacs and diets. At breakfast she drank truffle and celery soup washed down by hot chocolate. . . .

Pompadour's natural passion was fired by the arts, particularly the art of interior decor. She sponsored the new Sèvres porcelain factory, and she commissioned the most expensive chocolate service in France. It was quite *à la mode*

Portrait of Madame Du Barry by Jean Baptiste A. Gautier-D'Agoty, eighteenth-century French. Louis XV's last mistress was accused of plying her lovers with chocolate to whip up their ardor. *Sterling and Francine Clark Art Institute, Williamstown, Massachusetts*

LE BAIN.

De la Lettre ou du Chocolat   J'ai le cœur bien plus délicat
Que préfére Madame ? Ah ma chére Justine,   Plus foible infiniment, helas ! que la poitrine.

I. H. F. inv. S. Freudeberg del   A. Romanet sculp. 1774

A Paris chés Buldet rue de Gesvres.

now for elegant hostesses to order special pots and cups from great French porcelain makers like Sèvres—the pots with a *molinet* opening, the cups higher and narrower than coffee cups or teacups.

Highborn ladies began their day with a cup of chocolate in bed, for the good it might do them. As far back as 1679 their grandmothers had been told by Madame d'Aulnoy after her travels in Spain, "It is not surprising that Spanish women are thin, for there is nothing better than the chocolate which they drink to great excess. Furthermore, they season it inordinately with pepper and other spices as much as they are able, so that they do burn themselves." In the Louis XV era it was a gentler beverage flowing from those graceful pots into those slender cups. Until well into the century the liquid for chocolate was as likely to be beer or wine as water. Pepper and cloves were as reasonable a flavoring as sugar and vanilla. Musk and ambergris were still used. But about 1730 some mild English soul hit on the notion of dissolving chocolate in warm milk. This quieted version was taken up elsewhere—the first harbinger of Mom's after-school hot chocolate.

The next Louis, the tragic XVIth, ascended the French throne in 1774 with his frivolous queen, Marie Antoinette. Daughter of Austria's empress, Maria Theresia, she'd grown up with chocolate in Vienna. When marriage took her to Paris, her royal household included her personal chocolatier, who came up with novelties like chocolate mixed with powdered orchid bulbs (good for plumping out the figure charmingly); or scented with orange blossoms to soothe the nerves; with milk of almonds to bolster a delicate stomach.

It was the last chocolate frippery of Bourbon France, which had, as it were, married the cocoa bean. Marie Antoinette and Louis XVI went to the guillotine; the country endured the violent decades of its Revolution and then Napoleon. In 1814 the Bourbon monarchy was restored for a while under Louis XVIII, and the French resumed their peaceable absorptions—gastronomy, for example.

The Bath by Sigmund Freudenberger, late-eighteenth-century Swiss. This engraving evokes the familiar linkage of chocolate and the amorous emotions. In the French caption the maid asks, "The letter or the chocolate—which does madame prefer?" The languishing fair one replies, "Ah, my dear Justine, I have a heart much more delicate and infinitely weaker, alas! than my bosom." Highborn ladies like this one began their day with a cup of chocolate and, if fate was kind, a love letter. *The Metropolitan Museum of Art, New York, Harris Brisbane Dick Fund, 1933*

5

Paean to the Drink, Welcome to the Nibble

*D*uring *the years of Napoleon and the Restoration, a legal magistrate named Jean-Anthelme Brillat-Savarin rose high in his profession while in every spare minute he worked passionately at his avocation—the writing of witty theorizings, anecdotes, historical vignettes, and culinary opinions, which he called his "gastronomic meditations." In 1825 he published them as a book,* The Physiology of Taste, *a masterpiece in the literature of food. It included a chapter on chocolate,*

Madame Brion by Jacques André Joseph Aved (1750), Flemish/French. Rare instance of a *bourgeoise*—someone neither aristocratic nor glamorous nor enticing—pictured drinking chocolate. "When the weight of age makes itself felt," Brillat-Savarin suggested his "chocolate of the afflicted" as a restorative. *Private Collection*

43

Breakfast, engraving by Lépicié, after a painting by François Boucher, eighteenth-century French. The serving-man is pouring out chocolate from its typical pot. "When you have breakfasted well and copiously," Brillat-Savarin said, "if you swallow a generous cup of good chocolate at the end of the meal, you will have digested everything perfectly three hours later." *The Metropolitan Museum of Art, New York, The Elisha Whittelsey Fund, 1950*

which was still only drinking chocolate. He wrote:

> Time and experience, those two great teachers, have conclusively proved that chocolate, when carefully prepared, is a wholesome and agreeable form of food; that it is nourishing and easily digestible . . . that it is very suitable for persons faced with great mental exertion, preachers, lawyers, and above all travelers; and finally that it agrees with the feeblest stomachs, has proved beneficial in cases of chronic illness, and remains the last resource in diseases of the pylorus [the opening between stomach and intestine]. . . .

When you have breakfasted well and copiously [on a small meat pie, a cutlet, or a broiled kidney], if you swallow a generous cup of good chocolate at the end of the meal, you will have digested everything perfectly three hours later, and you will be able to dine in comfort. . . . Out of zeal for science, and by dint of eloquence, I have persuaded a good many ladies to try this experiment, although they protested that it would kill them; in every case they were delighted with the result. . . .

Brillat-Savarin grew eloquent when he came to the subject of "ambered" chocolate. He was not speaking of amber, the semiprecious gemstone, but of something perhaps still odder as a flavoring: ambergris, a waxlike substance taken from the intestine of the sperm whale. It is dotted with yellow and black spots, according to France's culinary encyclopedia, *Larousse Gastronomique,* and has "a strong and pleasant smell" (it is blended into many modern perfumes). Ambergris had long been used in European drinking chocolate, and even longer as an antispasmodic remedy. It was also much esteemed as an aphrodisiac, which made its relationship to chocolate like that of coals to Newcastle, considering chocolate's age-old liaison with the erotic, from Montezuma to Pompadour. That lady had, in fact, laced her self-encouraging chocolate with ambergris. But Brillat-Savarin—who, after all, was seventy when he published his book—was thinking of ambergris's other reputation, as a tonic:

When I get one of those days when the weight of age makes itself felt, or when one's mind is sluggish, I add a knob of ambergris the size of a bean, pounded with sugar, to a strong cup of chocolate, and I always find my condition improves marvelously. The burden of life becomes lighter, thoughts flow with ease, and I do not suffer from insomnia. . . .

Let any man who has drunk too deeply of the cup of pleasure, or given to work a notable portion of the time which should belong to sleep; who finds his wit temporarily losing its edge, the atmosphere humid, time dragging, and the air hard to breathe, or who is tortured by a fixed idea which robs him of all freedom of thought; let such a man, we say, administer to himself a good pint of ambered chocolate, allowing between sixty and seventy-two grains of amber to a pound, and he will see wonders. In my own peculiar way of specifying things, I call ambered chocolate "the chocolate of the afflicted." . . .

In *our* peculiar way, we might call it a tranquilizer.

"Being ourselves very fond of chocolate," as Brillat-Savarin confessed, he recommended it equally for the unafflicted. It was excellent, presumably without ambergris, "for our morning breakfasts, delights us at dinner with our creams,

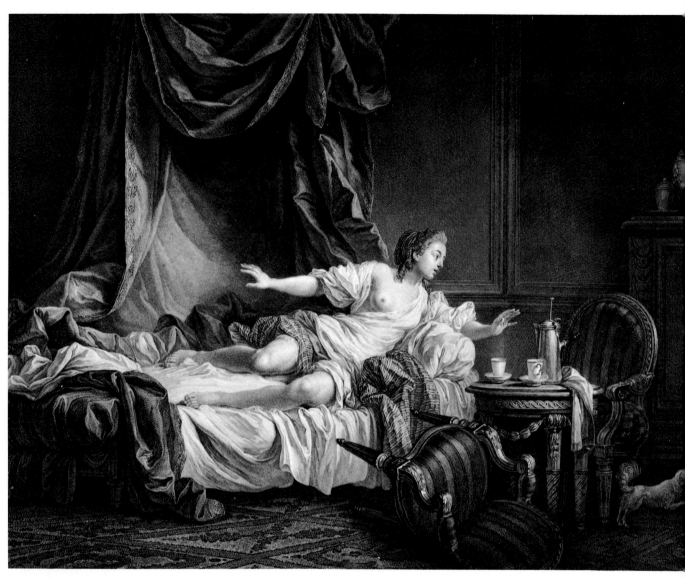

Fear by Noël Le Mire, eighteenth-century French. Something or someone has startled the lady at her morning chocolate. Brillat-Savarin evenhandedly advised a breakfast cup for all the ladies, to lose weight or to gain it. *Sterling and Francine Clark Art Institute, Williamstown, Massachusetts*

and enchants us yet again at the end of the evening with our ices, and sweets, and other drawing-room dainties. . . ."

An early advocate of dieting for health and beauty, the magistrate promoted chocolate for both losing and gaining weight. He told the chubby, "If you must have something sweet after dinner, choose a chocolate custard. . . . For breakfast, the inevitable rye bread, and chocolate rather than coffee." Yet he noted evenhandedly, "Every thin woman wants to put on flesh." She should, therefore, "Before eight o'clock in the morning, and in bed if necessary, drink a bowl of soup thickened with bread or noodles . . . or, if preferred, a cup of good chocolate."

This accommodating manysidedness of chocolate had been remarked by

Brillat-Savarin's countrywoman of a century and a half before, the celebrated Madame de Sévigńe, who won everlasting literary fame because she wrote such engrossing letters. In one of them she related, "I took chocolate night before last to digest my dinner in order to have a good supper. I took some yesterday for sustenance so that I might fast until evening. It had all the effects on me that I wanted; that is why I find chocolate agreeable, because it acts according to one's wishes."

Gourmets—called *gourmands* then by the French—made the best companions, Brillat-Savarin said, and he lovingly described the female type: "Those whose gourmandism consists chiefly of a love of sweet things have finer features, a more delicate air, neater figures, and above all, a very special way with their tongues."

By "sweet things" he meant pastries, creams, preserves. Chocolate was still mainly a drink, though Brillat-Savarin alluded to it a couple of times as a flavoring in food; that slenderizing chocolate custard, for instance. But, wise as always, he knew that better times were coming. Science would find new substances, he wrote, "like cacao, with new alimentary resources." And among the twenty "Aphorisms" that open his book is this one: "The discovery of a new dish does more for the happiness of mankind than the discovery of a star." Brillat-Savarin published his book in 1825. Three years later, though he didn't live to see it—he died in 1826, at the age of seventy-one—the happiness of mankind was enhanced when the first step was taken toward the discovery of eating chocolate.

It began with the quest for a better beverage. From the start, people had often found chocolate rather rich for comfortable drinking. When cocoa beans are ground, the essence produced is 53 to 55 percent cocoa butter, its natural vegetable fat. To cut the unctuousness, the Aztecs had stirred in corn flour. The eighteenth-century English used potato starch, arrowroot, and even powdered seashells. Once started on the idea of admixture, they went on to other substances for other effects, such as deepening the color of chocolate with a touch of red pigment, iron rust, or brick dust—until George III imposed fines or confiscation on the guilty (who usually bribed their way out). In England and Germany both, strange hybrids were sold: oatmeal chocolate, acorn chocolate . . . barley, Icelandic-moss, or rice chocolate . . .

Probably the very richness of real chocolate was the reason why physicians and laymen over the years had pronounced it so "nourishing." But now people wanted a lighter drink, and in 1828 a Dutch chemist named Coenraad van Houten found it for them. He invented a screw press that squeezed out about two-thirds of the cocoa butter and left "chocolate powder"—or, as it has been known ever since, cocoa—the basis of a drink with almost all the familiar savor of chocolate but none of the overrichness. Actually, defatted chocolate had probably been known earlier. In France, in the middle of the previous century, Diderot's *Encyclopédie* had printed an illustration showing a chocolate workshop with a screw press. But nothing much had been heard of that one, while van

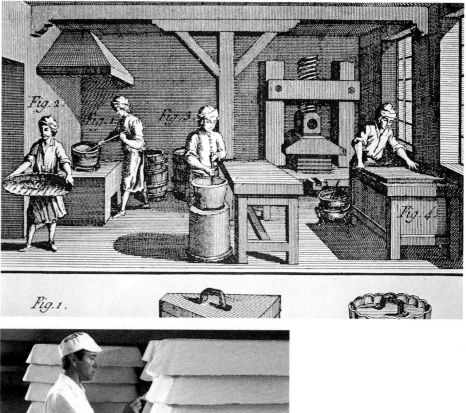

Illustration from Diderot's *Encyclopédie* showing an eighteenth-century French chocolate workshop with a screw press (*rear*). But it was a Dutch press invented in 1828 that finally led to the development of eating chocolate. *Copyright, CHOCOSUISSE, Switzerland*

Cocoa butter, pressed out and solidified. The new ingredient turned dry, bitter drinking chocolate into a happy nibble. *Copyright, CHOCOSUISSE, Switzerland*

Houten patented his device and enthralled Europe with it. He had done away with the need for starches and other thickeners. Next he ended the coloring agents by inventing the process, called "dutching" in his honor, still in use today. Cocoa is treated with alkali to neutralize its acidity, mellow its color and flavor, and render it more soluble in liquids.

Van Houten had done something else. The new manufacture of cocoa powder yielded all those extracted heaps of ivory-colored, glossy, fragrant, too-good-to-waste cocoa butter. On the other hand, the paste ground from cocoa beans, called "cocoa liquor" in the trade—*liquor* in the old sense, meaning liq-

The new cup of chocolate was more likely to be cocoa—served, in this advertising poster, by a new "Chocolate Girl" (see page 32). *Courtesy, Suchard-Tobler S.A., Switzerland*

uid essence, not alcohol—had always hardened into a chocolate too dry and bitter to be chewed with any enjoyment. Chocolate-house London had had a vogue for chocolate-laced cakes "in the Spanish style"; an English company in 1826 advertised chocolate lozenges as "a pleasant and nutritious substitute for food while travelling or when unusual fasting is caused by an irregular period of mealtimes"; and Brillat-Savarin mentioned chocolate as a food flavoring. But as a mouthful straight, just for the pleasure of it? Chocolate makers considered those heaps of cocoa butter. They pondered. Richness, undesirable in a drink, might be exceedingly desirable in something to eat. If cocoa butter were added, mellowing, softening, to chocolate liquor and sugar ... And, lo, these latter-day Quetzalcoatls gave a new gift unto the eager multitudes.

The first to do it were the English. The Bristol firm of Fry & Sons, which had been producing the drinking variety since 1728, introduced "eating chocolate" in 1847. It was grainy and rather harsh-flavored compared with the wonders yet to come. But the people of 1847 had never tasted anything like it, and they were enchanted. The reign of the world's happiest nibble had begun. Enter the Swiss at last, latecomers in the pageant. As recently as 1797 the immortal German author Goethe hadn't ventured on a trip to chocolate-poor Switzerland without taking along his own chocolate and chocolate pot from home. But when the Swiss took over, they really took over. By the end of the nineteenth century they would be stars.

The names unroll like chocolate fanfares. In 1819 François-Louis Cailler, having learned chocolate making as an apprentice in Italy, went home to Vevey and opened Switzerland's first chocolate factory, complete with machines he invented to improve his product. In 1809 twelve-year-old Philipp Suchard saw chocolate for the first time when his ailing mother asked him to pick up a pound of it as a tonic from a Neuchâtel apothecary—at a price equal to three days' pay for a workman. In 1826 he started making chocolate in an old mill powered by a water wheel, with a mechanical grinder he designed; in 1893 his trademark became the first registered with the International Patents Office. Charles-Amédée Kohler, son of a Swiss cocoa-bean importer, began operations in 1831; it was he who first thought of a delectable enduring fillip: blending finely ground hazelnuts into chocolate.

So far, Swiss chocolate firsts had all taken place in the French-speaking part of the country. In 1845 Rodolphe Sprüngli-Amman set up shop in Zurich and became the pioneer for German-speaking Switzerland. A couple of French Swiss, Daniel Peter and Henri Nestlé, in 1875 invented—large flourish of trumpets here—milk chocolate. About the same time, Rodolphe Lindt of Berne, a German Swiss again, developed the technique for creating "fondant" chocolate so caressingly smooth that it literally melted in your mouth. In 1884 in Montreux Alexis Séchaud debuted; in 1913 his company would devise filled chocolate, paving the way for those most sophisticated of bonbons, chocolate-covered liqueurs. After decades as a confectionary seller in Berne, in 1899 Jean Tobler became a manufacturer, with his own masterful line of ever more opulent chocolate bars and boxed assortments.

With all this going on, with chocolate getting better and better, more tastable, more melting, more *eatable,* a blandished humankind clamored for more cocoa beans. Which meant that the great worldwide spread of cocoa-tree cultivation was on.

Photos, Copyright, CHOCOSUISSE, Switzerland

The Swiss
Founding Fathers—
A Chocolate Fanfare of Names

François-Louis Cailler

Philipp Suchard

Rodolphe Sprüngli-Amman

Daniel Peter

Henri Nestlé

Rodolphe Lindt

Jean Tobler

6

Growing
Cocoa Beans

*U*ntil about 1700 Spain had controlled the supply of cocoa beans, with its plantations in Central America. By the turn of the century French plantings on the West Indian island of Martinique filled some of France's needs. Even so, in 1810 Spanish-held Venezuela alone still produced half the world's cocoa, and the Spanish drank up one-third of the entire world crop. It didn't leave much for everyone else in the about-to-explode chocolate era. So everyone else in the nineteenth century set

Both green and ripe-colored pods together decorate any one tree. *Courtesy, Société des Produits Nestlé S.A., Vevey, Switzerland*

about growing their own: the Dutch in Ceylon, Java, Sumatra, and Timor; the Belgians in the Congo; the English in the West Indies; the Germans in the Cameroons; and the French added the East African island of Madagascar to Martinique.

The Portuguese, now firmly in control of Brazil, planted seeds from its cocoa trees (a legacy from that long-ago French incursion) on São Thomé and Principe, twin islands off the west coast of Africa. During the 1890s Europe's appetite for chocolate stimulated the founding of still more plantations on the little "chocolate islands," which became the leading cocoa producers, accounting for one-sixth of the global supply. The trouble was that their plantations were worked by indentured laborers from Angola on the African mainland, and in 1901 rumors began to reach Europe that they were not free workers but slaves.

About a third of the islands' crops was bought by English companies. Four of the most important of these—Cadbury, Fry, Rowntree, and Terry's—happened to be owned by Quaker families, with their humanitarian tradition. As a matter of fact, almost a century earlier the father of Cadbury's founder had worked to abolish slavery in British colonies. Now the Cadbury company decided to investigate the rumors of new slavery in one of their own supply areas. William Cadbury, representing the third generation of his family in the chocolate business, was put in charge of the matter in 1903. For the next six years he pursued his inquiries in Lisbon with the Portuguese government, and in the islands. He got the support of the Rowntree and Fry companies in England and

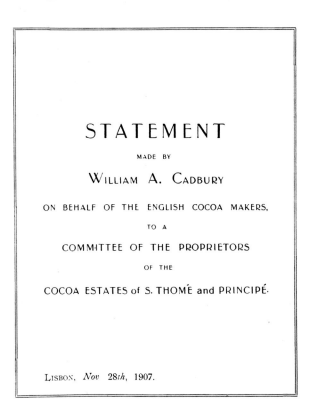

Cadbury's original press release. *Courtesy, Cadbury Limited*

STATEMENT

MADE BY

WILLIAM A. CADBURY

ON BEHALF OF THE ENGLISH COCOA MAKERS,

TO A

COMMITTEE OF THE PROPRIETORS

OF THE

COCOA ESTATES of S. THOMÉ and PRINCIPÉ.

LISBON, *Nov* 28*th*, 1907.

Stollwerk in Germany (no American firm was willing to join in) as he verified for himself the workers' "ghastly conditions" and "the illegal and brutal system of forcibly recruiting labour in Angola," then preventing the men from ever returning home.

During all that time Cadbury, guided by the British Foreign Office, kept trying to persuade the Portuguese government and plantation owners to correct the abuses voluntarily. On November 28, 1907, William Cadbury addressed a meeting of proprietors of plantations on São Thomé and Principe "on behalf of the English cocoa makers." His remarks were published in a press release for English newspapers and read in part:

> In one of your best managed estates the doctor states that most of the mortality is from two diseases—anaemia and dysentery; complaints that are easily developed by people in a depressed mental condition. It is also admitted that the highest death rate is among the newly arrived labourers, and this is exactly what one would expect when we know that these people are forcibly taken from their homes for work across the sea, without any hope of return.... There is no repatriation to Angola: the ships that go to the islands crowded with labourers carry none back to their homes. Until the present state of things is changed no argument will persuade the world that this is free labour....
>
> When the system of repatriation is established and men and women and children are actually returned to their homes, they will inspire their friends with confidence in the S. Thomé plantations, and the islands would no longer be regarded as the grave from which no man returns.... The returned native would be the best recruiting agent for new volunteers who would go with light heart to the islands, because they would know that at the end of their contract they would return with money to their friends.... The labourer will be kept in better health and spirits by the prospect of return....
>
> The abuses which are still taking place ... are I believe ... the last traces of a bad system that you all deplore, and will, I believe, remove with a strong hand, so that it shall not be possible to associate the name of slavery with that of your great nation.
>
> We have always been buyers of S. Thomé cocoa, and in the hope of continuing for many years your business friends, we respectfully urge upon you the need for reforms.... Much as we should regret to lose the opportunity of buying your excellent cocoa, and even knowing that it would entail to us financial loss, speaking at least for my own firm, our conscience would not allow us to go on purchasing raw material for our business, unless we are assured that in the future it is to be produced by free labour.

We plead for strong and immediate action, and confidently trust that the agriculturists, who have by their courage and energy done so much in one generation to raise the island of S. Thomé to a colony of the foremost rank, will assist their able administrators to banish from their estates the remnants of a bad system, and establish in the ancient colony of Angola a standard of true freedom, worthy of the nation which first explored the shores of Africa, and is counted among the greatest colonising Powers of the earth.

Despite Cadbury's persuasive speech, island conditions remained unchanged, and in March 1909 the Cadbury company announced that it would no longer buy Portuguese cocoa. Other chocolate firms in Europe and America joined the boycott. In 1910 William Cadbury published a book about the affair, *Labour in Portuguese West Africa,* and a couple of years later conditions did improve on São Thomé and Principe. But by then the boycott had reduced the islands' role in the cocoa trade. The Cadbury company, for example, had switched its purchases to British West Africa. There, in what is now the republic of Ghana, seeds were planted from São Thomé, Principe, and the neighboring Spanish-owned island of Fernando Po, whose trees were descended from the Aztec seeds planted by Cortés centuries before. In Ghana young trees were sprouting into the major cocoa plantations of the future.

European growers of the cocoa tree needed several things: first, enough political or economic influence over a territory to move in with plantations; second, specific conditions of geography and climate. The cocoa tree thrives in latitudes lying between ten degrees south and ten degrees north of the equator—at most, twenty degrees north and south of it—where the temperature is usually at least eighty degrees Fahrenheit and never falls below sixty. There can't be much wind; the slender trees could not withstand it. There should be loose soil and screened sunlight; the original wild cocoas grew up in the shade of larger trees like the banana in the Central American forests. Finally, the cocoa needs rainfall, abundant and more or less steady, at least fifty inches a year.

The conditions were met in a number of places, and in the nineteenth century plantations spread from Brazil to São Thomé, from Venezuela to the Philippines, Madagascar to Ceylon. Everywhere the growing and harvesting methods were pretty much the same, and not significantly different from either what they had been in Montezuma's time or would be in the 1980s.

Cocoa trees can grow as tall as fifty feet, as old as sixty years. Generally, though, they're kept pruned to about twenty-five feet, for easier gathering of the bean pods, and they reach the limit of their productivity at thirty or forty years. The trees demonstrate the life force triumphant, fairly pulsing with growth vitality, putting forth leaves, flowers, and fruit (the bean pods) all the time, and all together. And they do it eccentrically. Since the year-round freight of rather large leaves is burden enough for the fragile branches, the bean pods grow directly on the trunk and thicker main branches, up to thirty at any given

Botanical drawing shows the cocoa tree's leaf, flower, pod, and seeds within. All grow on the tree at the same time—all the time. *Courtesy, Société des Produits Nestlé S.A., Vevey, Switzerland*

Pods and flowers grow, eccentrically, right on the trunk. *Courtesy, Société des Produits Nestlé S.A., Vevey, Switzerland*

time. So do the flowers, up to a hundred thousand blossoms a year. All in glorious color. The flowers are baby-pink and white; the young leaves, depending on the type of cocoa tree, vary from pale green to lavender to purple, then all mature to dark green; the football-shaped pods ripen from green to either yellow or red, again depending on the variety of tree, with both green and ripe-colored pods decorating any tree at any one time. A stand of cocoa trees, then, is a visual treat. But not a sniffably chocolate one. The tantalizing aroma develops later. At the growing phase even the delicate blossoms are odorless.

There are two main general classifications of cocoa tree: Forastero, cultivated mostly in Brazil and West Africa, and Criollo, the Central American native. The first produces a dark, purplish bean, rather harsh in flavor, but hardy and easy to grow for high yield. The Criollo tree is lower-yielding, more susceptible to problems of disease and weather, and more difficult to grow; but its yellowish-white bean is finer and milder in flavor. The Forastero is known as the "base bean"; it makes up 90 percent of the world crop and forms the bulk of most finished chocolate. The Criollo, rarer and more expensive, is the "flavor bean." It is blended into every fine chocolate in a ratio determined by the manufacturer's recipe—and the product's price. Both the Forastero and Criollo classifications include a number of varieties as well as hybrids, each christened for its home area, such as Guayaquil, Accra, Bahia, and Caracas.

To provide the shaded sunlight cocoa trees love, the endearingly named "cocoa mothers" are planted right alongside. Tropical forest trees like the banana, baobab, cassava, and pimiento protect the tender young cocoas from too

Seedlings are started in shaded rush baskets, then transplanted near "cocoa mothers." *Courtesy, Société des Produits Nestlé S.A., Vevey, Switzerland*

much sun, especially during the vulnerable first three or four years. Then the trees start producing their fruit, the bean pods reaching peak yield at about eight years and maintain it for the next three decades. Though the pods grow on their tree trunks every day of every month, and in some places harvesting goes on all year, most plantations bring order to this heedless teeming. They generally harvest twice a year, at the beginning and at the end of the rainy season. The ripe pod, about eight inches long and three or four inches around, is cut down carefully by hand so as not to injure younger pods still ripening on the tree. The crop goes off to the next stage, at a nearby fermentation site.

Here, with a knife or just a quick blow with a stick, the tough pods are split open to reveal the cocoa beans, twenty to forty per pod. They look rather like almonds, embedded in a sticky white pulp. The beans are bitter-tasting at this point, but the pulp is delicious. Undoubtedly it was the sticky stuff those pre-Columbian monkeys and birds were after when they foraged in the wild trees. Children in cocoa-growing areas still munch dreamily on the pulp from freshly opened pods, and their mothers use it to make lovely soft drinks and dessert jellies. Most of the pulp, though, is scooped out right along with the beans, and the whole mass is set out to ferment. The method used today seems unchanged from a past century. Banana leaves are laid on the ground; the beans

Ripe pods are cut down carefully by hand. *Copyright, CHOCOSUISSE, Switzerland*

are spread over them, covered with a second layer of banana leaves, and left to ferment for several days, turned around occasionally to make sure the fermentation is even. Sometimes the process takes place in baskets instead of on the ground; sometimes, the most modern method, in large, flat, sloping boxes, under a layer of leaves.

Now at last a glimmering sense of chocolate emerges. During fermentation the beans, helped along by the 113-degree heat generated by the disintegrating pulp around them, develop chemical elements known as "flavor precursors."

At a nearby fermentation site each pod is split open to reveal the cocoa beans.
Courtesy, Société des Produits Nestlé S.A., Vevey, Switzerland

Copyright, CHOCOSUISSE, Switzerland

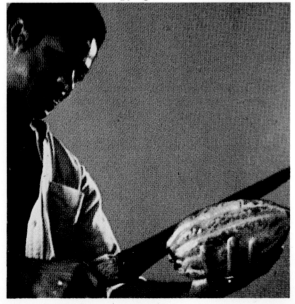

The beans are dried in the tropical sun. *Copyright, Cacaofabriek De Zaan B.V. 1984, Holland*

Packed in jute bags, the dried beans are shipped to chocolate factories everywhere. *Courtesy, Société des Produits Nestlé S.A., Vevey, Switzerland*

The beans lose the worst of their bitterness and begin changing from lavender or white to brown, the expected chocolate color. Without fermenting, no matter what other processes they went through later, cocoa beans could never develop the expected chocolate taste, though the flavor precursors themselves are still not much like it.

As the beans ferment, their moisture keeps drip-drip-dripping away for as long as a week. Even so, they end up 60 percent water—making them not only wastefully heavy to ship, but liable to spoil during the voyage. So next they're spread out to dry in the tropical sun for several days (but moved under protective overhangs at night and during showers). Their color gets browner still, their aroma a little closer to chocolate, their moisture content down to a manageable 5 to 7 percent. They are ready to be packed into jute bags, 140 pounds or so at a time, and sent across various oceans to chocolate factories everywhere.

7

Founding Factories

*E*verywhere is the word for chocolate factories
in the nineteenth century. With the invention
of eating chocolate they seemed to blossom as
abundantly as the cocoa tree itself, and most
of them are bywords to this day. In England, of course,
there was J. S. Fry & Sons, the original introducer of
eating chocolate in 1847. There was also a young man
named John Cadbury. In 1824 he opened a tea and coffee
shop in Birmingham, and soon branched out to chocolate,
which he made himself, from roasting the beans to

Old package shows cocoa tree's leaf, flower, and pods. *Courtesy, Cadbury Limited*

Drawing of Cadbury's original factory (1879). *Courtesy, Cadbury Limited*

grinding them with mortar and pestle. Gradually the chocolate took over so thoroughly that by 1849, two years after Fry, the Cadbury family was selling eating chocolate from a larger shop in Birmingham. Thirty years later they expanded still further and built a large factory in nearby Bournville. Another company had been making chocolate since 1785; it grew into Rowntree, still famous in England and abroad. Terry's of York, which had been in the candy business since 1767, sniffed the cocoa-scented breeze in the mid-nineteenth century and added chocolate to their line; in 1886 they built their own factory and achieved renown.

In Germany B. Sprengel began operations in 1851, and almost every city boasted a chocolate factory: Stollwerk in Cologne, Hildebrand in Berlin, David in Halle. In France Menier got started; in Holland, Blooker, Bensdorp, Droste, and Van Houten. And that Swiss fanfare of names rolled out: Cailler, Suchard, Nestlé, Tobler . . .

A Swiss working in Austria had given the world its favorite chocolate painting, *La Belle Chocolatière,* in 1743. The next year Vienna's chocolate makers

...urtesy, Bensdorp B.V. Cacao-en Chocoladefabrieken, Holland

Suchard factory around the turn of the century. *Courtesy, Suchard-Tobler S.A., Switzerland*

Courtesy, Suchard-Tobler S.A., Switzerland

Courtesy, Suchard-Tobler S.A., Switzerland

Bensdorp factory. *Courtesy, Bensdorp B.V. Cacao-en Chocoladefabrieken, Holland*

were numerous enough to organize a kind of guild. They produced a dozen different varieties—for pleasure drinking and for medicinal use—and their reputation was high, with other European countries importing their creations. In the 1820s Goethe (whose fondness for chocolate has already been noted here) was vacationing in the Austrian spa resort of Karlsbad. Over seventy years old by then, but chipper, he sent a gift package to Ulrike von Levetzow, the nineteen-year-old girl he adored. In the box were several geological samples and some chocolate—the fine Viennese kind, he emphasized in a note. And the great poet added a fond little couplet:

> *Enjoy this whenever it suits your mood,*
> *Not as a drink but as a much-loved food!*

Goethe, then, is one of history's earliest recorded nibblers of chocolate. Apparently, decades before the invention of the edible form, people were biting into the tablets meant for dissolving in a drink. We can only assume that at least one of the dozen Viennese chocolate varieties had some sugar blended in.

Vienna soon lost its export eminence to the Swiss and the Dutch with their innovative machines and processes. Locally cherished brands kept the standard up, but the city never did produce a world-class brand of chocolate candy. Instead it came up with the world's most famous chocolate cake, the Sacher torte, the only name in the chocolate pantheon that belongs not to a factory but a hotel.

Courtesy, Société des Produits Nestlé S.A., Vevey, Switzerland

Courtesy, Société des Produits Nestlé S.A., Vevey, Switzerland

Courtesy, Société des Produits Nestlé S.A., Vevey, Switzerland

Courtesy, Société des Produits Nestlé S.A., Vevey, Switzerland

Goethe in Heidelberg by Hermann Junker, nineteenth-century German. A lifelong drinker of chocolate, the great poet in old age was one of its earliest recorded nibblers.

Pastrycooks were a little slow to take up baking with chocolate, which, after all, had been known in cake-happy Vienna since 1711. It wasn't until 1778 that a cookbook gave a recipe for a *"Schiocolati* Torte," composed of ground almonds, cinnamon, cloves, ginger, and lemon peel as well as grated chocolate; evidently the cocoa bean was still thought of in association with strong spices. A curious Viennese concoction of the time combined chocolate with flour browned in fat and salted; then milk was stirred in and the whole thing poured over softened slices of bread. (Which was no more curious than a colonial American breakfast porridge made by thickening chocolate with cassava, a starchy tuber.) Vienna got closer to Sacher torte with a prefiguring chocolate-cake recipe in a 1799 cookbook called *The Viennese Sugar Baker.* In that one the spices dropped out, leaving the chocolate, sugar, and eggs to shine forth unalloyed.

The original building of the Hotel Sacher as it appeared in 1869. *Courtesy, Austrian National Tourist Office*

Finally, in 1832 a sixteen-year-old apprentice chef named Franz Sacher put together the elements for the cake that would make his name one of three signifying Vienna forevermore (the other two being Johann Strauss and Sigmund Freud). Young Sacher was employed in the household of Austria's imperial chancellor, Prince Metternich. It was there that he composed his cake—a rich chocolate batter, plus an apricot-jam glaze and a glossy chocolate frosting—and it was there, on the prince's table, that it first appeared. Probably it began to be called Sacher torte when Franz, several aristocratic jobs later, took his recipe with him into the delicatessen and hotel he opened in 1849. The cake was a lip-smacking success, sold and served in Sacher's new businesses. Franz's son Eduard opened a grander hotel of his own in 1876, the Hotel Sacher, opposite the Vienna Opera, legendary and still glamorously alive today. Eduard, too, served Sacher torte, a lot of Sacher torte. By 1888 he was telling a Viennese newspaper that he portioned out four hundred cakes a day to diners at his hotel. More Sacher tortes were mailed to Paris, Berlin, London, even overseas. The cake was copied by bakers around the world. In its own way Sacher became as beloved a chocolate name as Nestlé, Suchard, and Hershey. It was to have a long and eventful life, whose later history we will encounter in due course.

In the United States, Walter Baker in 1820 took over the company his grandfather had founded on the Neponset River in the previous century. A firm and early believer in advertising, he used it to expand the business. After the Civil War Baker's acquired the right to put Liotard's "Chocolate Girl" on its packages and ads. To this day Americans are often astonished to learn that the painting exists as anything but Baker's trademark.

Other long-lived companies began: Maillard in 1848, for instance. Today the company is known for its chocolate bars, but back then it concentrated on cocoa and even ran a "chocolate school," with free lessons on properly preparing the drink. Cocoa powder was already available in tins, with cooking instructions on the wrapping, but an 1851 cookbook called *The American Matron* had a better idea: "Purchase the nut as imported in bags, roast it, as coffee, and crack it in a mortar. Then boil it well in water. Doubtless the real cocoa taste is obtained in this way and you are sure to get a pure article." It is, and you are. As recently as the 1960s (and probably even now) a similar procedure was followed in rural Puerto Rico. Some farms were lucky enough to have a few cocoa trees. No one cultivated them; no one knew when or how they'd gotten there. (Hernán Cortés's plant-as-you-sail policy seems a likely explanation.) The farm wife would gather ripe pods, give the pulp to the children, and spread the beans

"Friar Drinking Chocolate" by Jose M. Oropeza, 1891, Mexican. Latin Americans still make their beverage with straight chocolate, not cocoa powder. *Museo Nacional de Historia, Mexico*

71

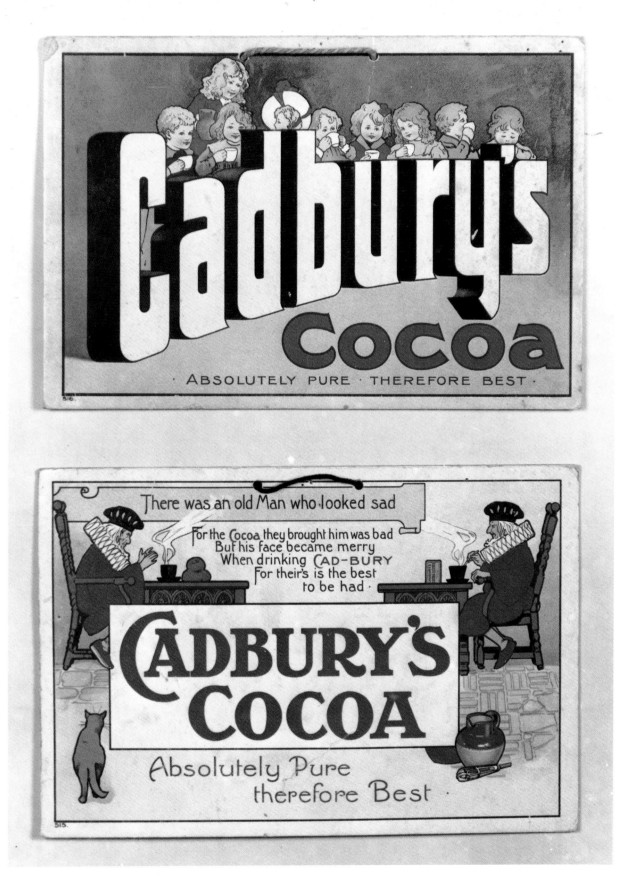

Courtesy, Cadbury Limited

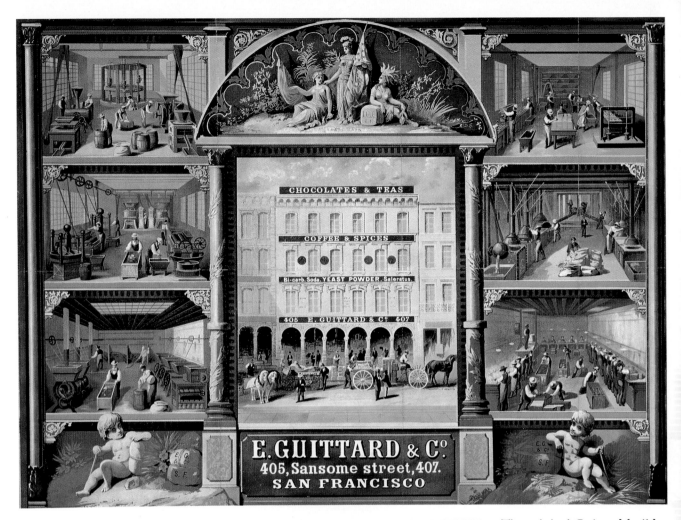

The original Guittard building surrounded by drawings showing the manufacture of chocolate. *Courtesy, Guittard Chocolate Company, Burlingame, California*

Old packages. *Courtesy, Guittard Chocolate Company, Burlingame, California*

on her sunny roof to ferment and dry for several days. Then she'd roast the beans in a large pot over her open wood fire, put them through her coffee grinder, and serve up a drink more delicious than any other hot chocolate anywhere, according to those who have tasted it.

The American Matron had good reason to advise do-it-yourself cocoa. The same year that the cookbook was published, 1851, the distinguished British medical journal *Lancet* ran an analysis of fifty commercial cocoas, showing that

Illustration from Brockhaus's encyclopedia, late nineteenth century, Germany. Under the heading **CHOCOLATE MANUFACTURE** the machines for various steps in the process are shown: 1. Hammering table (where the loosened shells of the roasted cocoa beans were knocked off). 2. Mixer with fixed refining stones. 3. Grinding machine. 4. Press (to extract cocoa butter). 5. Mixer with rotating refining stones. 6. Machine to knock out air bubbles. 7. Steam-driven roasting machine. 8. Molding apparatus. 9. Unmechanized roaster.

CHOKOLADENFABRIKATION.

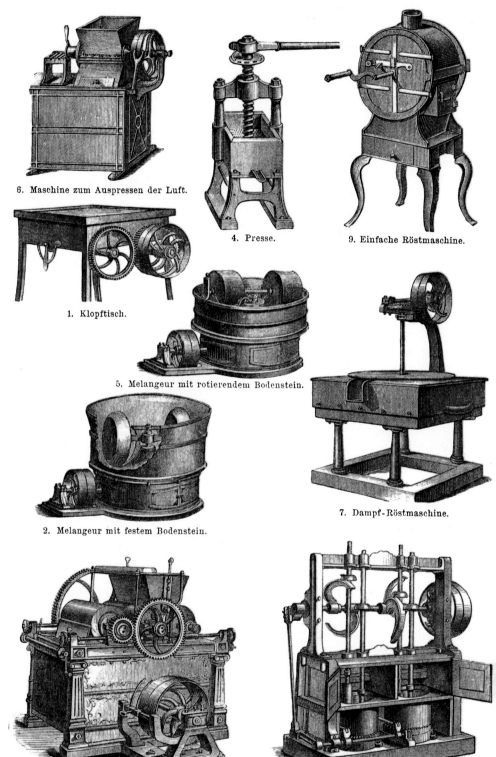

6. Maschine zum Auspressen der Luft.

1. Klopftisch.

4. Presse.

9. Einfache Röstmaschine.

5. Melangeur mit rotierendem Bodenstein.

2. Melangeur mit festem Bodenstein.

7. Dampf-Röstmaschine.

3. Schleif- oder Reibmaschine.

Brockhaus' Conversations-Lexikon. 13. Aufl.

8. Stampfwerk.

Zu Artikel: Chokolade.

90 percent of them were adulterated, mostly with starchy filler or lead pigment. Even after all of van Houten's work on defatting and dutching, bad habits died hard, it seemed, at least in England. There was an exception, though. Cadbury prided itself on making "pure product" cocoa, innocent of fillers.

Cocoa was still an important product; but Cadbury, like the other companies, was increasingly occupied with chocolate for eating. In 1857 the oldest of today's great Belgian bonbon makers got started when Neuhaus opened a boutique in Brussels. In the United States William Loft, son of an English candy maker, opened his and the nation's first retail chocolate-candy shop in 1860. The new thing about Loft's was that instead of being a chocolate manufacturer it was a purveyor of bonbons, molding them from chocolate purchased in bulk. The idea was successful, and Loft's grew into a large chain of stores throughout New York, New Jersey, and Connecticut.

On the other side of the country, also in 1860, the foundation was laid for a company that would be the opposite side of the chocolate coin from Loft's. That year Etienne Guittard left France and his job in a chocolate factory to go gold prospecting in San Francisco. After three years he hadn't found any gold. But he had brought from France a supply of fine chocolate to barter for prospecting gear. The shopkeepers he traded with assured him that there was a future for him and his wonderful chocolate in San Francisco. Guittard went back to France, where he worked and saved to buy the equipment he would need. In 1868 he sailed for San Francisco again, and opened the business that developed into one of the important American manufacturers of top-grade chocolate for wholesale customers. Some of the country's best confectioners, bakers, and ice-cream makers (Baskin-Robbins, for one) use Guittard.

Ghirardelli is another company that got its start in the California gold rush and is prominent today. Domingo Ghirardelli set up tents in the gold fields to sell a variety of goods to the miners. With the capital he accumulated, in 1862 he went into the confectionery trade. By the turn of the century the firm was specializing in the manufacture of chocolate bars. It is still going strong, as both a wholesaler and a retailer.

Of all the companies that were springing up in the United States, one was to stand out ultimately as the name that any American would free-associate with the word *chocolate*. Like Suchard and Nestlé in Switzerland, it began as the name of a man. Milton Snavely Hershey had been in the sugar-candy and caramel business for a couple of decades when he visited the Chicago Exposition of 1893 and watched a demonstration of German chocolate-making machinery. At that moment Milton Hershey seemed to know that he had found his destiny. "Caramels are only a fad," he told a companion. "Chocolate is a permanent thing. I'm going to make chocolate." And so he did, gradually switching over his product line and in 1903 building a factory. But it was so much more than a factory—it was in fact a whole chocolate society—that we'll look at it separately, in closer detail, later on.

8

Making Chocolate

The machinery Milton Hershey saw in Chicago had been developing throughout the century. After Cortés brought back cocoa beans, for many years Europeans ground them into chocolate essentially the way the Aztecs had—that is, by hand. Usually in Europe and America the beans were crushed in mortar and pestle, sometimes between stone or porcelain disks. Later, waterwheels were used to power chocolate-grinding devices, by Dr. James Baker in Massachusetts, for instance, and Philipp

Courtesy, Société des Produits Nestlé S.A., Vevey, Switzerland

Suchard and Rodolphe Lindt in Switzerland. But by then James Watt had invented the steam engine, in 1765, and it wasn't long before chocolate mills were putting it to work. In 1780 the engine drove a grinding machine in a factory in Spain, European chocolate's homeland. In 1795 Fry & Sons (England's future eating-chocolate pioneers) ground cocoa beans by steam power for the first time. In the next century industrialization took over in chocolate as it did in everything else. "Steam Chocolate," one German brand was called, pointing proudly to its manufacturing process. The machinery that so impressed Milton Hershey in 1893 would be improved and sophisticated in coming decades. But, for the most part, modern chocolate manufacture had arrived.

The final refinement had come in 1879, when Rodolphe Lindt, looking to create the perfect chocolate, rich and smooth, came up with two luscious ideas. One had to do with cocoa butter and its unique character. Other vegetable fats melt at room temperature; cocoa butter stays firm up to ninety-two degrees Fahrenheit. Lindt found that by adding the right amount of extra cocoa butter he got chocolate that was delectably rich yet stayed neatly solid until it melted on the human tongue—whose normal temperature is, by delightful chance, above that same ninety-two degrees Fahrenheit. Lindt's second idea came to him as he hand-worked his chocolate in a narrow trough. The longer he kneaded and mixed, the smoother the mass got—the smooth, melting texture we taste today in the best chocolate. To achieve it more easily, Lindt invented equipment along lines still being followed. The process came to be called "conching," from the Spanish word *concha,* "shell," the shape of the earliest conching troughs.

Conching takes place well along in the production process, after a good many other steps. When we left the cocoa beans on page 61, they were still far away from being chocolate. They'd been fermented to develop flavor precursors, dried, and shipped off to factories. *There* they become chocolate.

First the beans are cleaned. Stones, jute fibers, sand, dust, bits of wood and pod are cleared away by sieves, electric brushes, and vacuum equipment. Then human inspectors discard any beans not perfectly fermented and dried. Screens sort the beans by size. The larger the bean, the longer the roast. And roasting is the next, crucial step.

It is roasting that brings out in cocoa beans the distinctive, beguiling chocolate aroma and taste, and incidentally makes the factory a magical place. In his fantasy for children, *Charlie and the Chocolate Factory,* British author Roald Dahl depicts a building that encloses candy meadows, a chocolate river, and a waterfall to do the mixing work. That's not exactly how a modern plant looks, with its businesslike machines, scientific gauges, and automated control panels. But Dahl's daydream and its real-life counterpart have one thing in common. As Dahl wrote, "And every time he went by, he would begin to walk very, very slowly, and he would hold his nose high in the air and take long deep sniffs of the gorgeous chocolatey smell all round him. Oh, how he loved that smell!"

The aura around a factory is gorgeous indeed, and it comes in good measure from the roasting beans. In a painstaking process the intensity of the roast is calculated to suit not only the variety of bean in the large ovens but the eventual product. Cocoa powder, for example, should have a stronger aroma, therefore longer-roasted beans; while different kinds of chocolate range from mild-flavored to strong, with the beans roasted accordingly, from fifteen to twenty minutes at 100 to 150 degrees Celsius. Whatever the intensity, the operator must be careful not to overdo it or the batch will be unusable for its intended purpose. It could even end up burned and completely worthless.

After the roast the beans are not only aromatic but darker in color. Their husks are dry and loosened, ready for the next step. A winnowing machine cracks open the beans, revealing the nibs inside, the basic material that will produce chocolate (little morsels so tasty now, roasted, that in present-day Mexico they are sometimes eaten out of hand). The loosened husks are blown away mechanically—but not thrown away; they are salvaged and used to make cattle feed, fertilizer, and some medicines—while the nibs go on to be blended. To get a precise nuance of flavor, a chocolate manufacturer will blend up to ten varieties of cocoa bean. The specific combination is every company's precious secret recipe.

The blended nibs are then ground by still another machine, which generates enough heat in the process to melt the cocoa-butter content. The result is chocolate liquor, a deep-colored chocolaty-smelling paste, which hardens as it cools. Properly shaped, and with no added ingredients except perhaps a bit of extra cocoa butter, this is sold as baking chocolate—about as pure as you can get.

Pure, but not really good to eat. Eating chocolate, even the relatively dry "extrabittersweet" flavor so praised by purists, needs more cocoa butter, some sugar, and further processing before it can be considered a treat. It begins with the chocolate liquor, made from beans that have been roasted and blended with cocoa powder in mind as the end product. The liquor is put under hydraulic pressure to extract most of the cocoa butter, leaving only 10 to 20 percent—as desired—in a dry press cake, which is pulverized and sieved. The resulting powder is cocoa. It can be combined with sugar and other flavorings to make the range of cocoa-drink mixes on the market. It can be left as it is, or dutched in the alkalizing procedure van Houten invented over a century and a half ago. The huge De Zaan cocoa company of Holland varies the dutching to achieve sixty different shadings from mild to strong-tasting, from light through reddish browns to almost black browns, according to the specifications of their commercial customers. Cocoa powder is used not only in the cup, but to flavor and color cookies (Oreos are made with cocoa), pastries, confections, puddings, cake mixes, ice creams . . .

A good deal of chocolate liquor does not become cocoa; it becomes chocolate. For this it needs the extra cocoa butter that flowed out as a liquid when the hydraulic machine produced cocoa press-cakes. The liquid is filtered to eliminate stray cocoa particles, and away from the hydraulic heat it hardens into gleaming ivory bars. Some of the cocoa butter is sold to manufacturers of skin

STEPS IN THE MANUFACTURE OF CHOCOLATE

Sorting the cocoa beans. *Courtesy, Société des Produits Nestlé S.A., Vevey, Switzerland*

Roasting. *Courtesy, Société des Produits Nestlé S.A., Vevey, Switzerland*

Winnowing away the shells. *Courtesy, Société des Produits Nestlé S.A., Vevey, Switzerland*

Grinding. *Courtesy, Société des Produits Nestlé S.A., Vevey, Switzerland*

Extracting the cocoa butter; cocoa press cakes emerge at right. *Copyright, CHOCOSUISSE, Switzerland*

White chocolate—all cocoa butter, no chocolate. *Copyright, CHOCOSUISSE, Switzerland*

Mixing. *Courtesy, Société des Produits Nestlé S.A., Vevey, Switzerland*

Refining. *Courtesy, Société des Produits Nestlé S.A., Vevey, Switzerland*

Conching. *Courtesy, Société des Produits Nestlé S.A., Vevey, Switzerland*

Tempering. *Courtesy, Société des Produits Nestlé S.A., Vevey, Switzerland*

Cadbury advertised its popularity with English firemen . . .
Courtesy, Cadbury Limited

oils and lotions, soaps and creams, products that it enhances with a beautiful emollience and a redolence of cocoa. Most of it, though, fulfills a higher calling: the greater glory of chocolate. Besides the lovely things it does for taste and texture, it also contributes to chocolate's great keeping qualities, because, unlike other fats, it almost never goes rancid. The amount added varies with the kind of chocolate being mixed, and with the individual companies' recipes. On the whole, cocoa-butter content increases as you go from extrabittersweet to sweet, from dark to light. The zenith is reached with white chocolate, which contains no chocolate liquor (that's why it's white) but is instead all cocoa butter, plus milk and sugar.

... and with Queen Victoria in the royal train. *Courtesy, Cadbury Limited*

The milk added to milk chocolate isn't a constant, either; it's not always the same kind of milk. Most factories used the dried form, since fluid milk turns the chocolate mixture too liquid. But Hershey in America, Cadbury in England, and Cailler in Switzerland do use fluid milk, condensed, possibly as an homage to their forebears. Cailler has long been merged with Nestlé as the deluxe member of the partnership, and Henri Nestlé started his business career by inventing both a baby formula and the condensed milk that went into it. When the Swiss chocolate maker Daniel Peter was developing milk chocolate, he found Nestlé's condensed milk perfect—that is, thick enough—for his mixture, and the two men built a company with the combination. As for Milton Hershey, when he set out to make milk chocolate in Pennsylvania's lush farm country he was determined to use fresh—not powdered—milk from the local cows. He, too, found a way of using condensed milk to get the chocolate he wanted. To this day the Hershey and Cailler recipes faithfully include condensed milk. Cadbury condenses milk collected from surrounding dairy farms. The practice seems only fitting for the leading manufacturer in England, where in 1730 someone first thought of drinking chocolate in milk instead of water.

Whatever the ingredients, they are kneaded together in the next machine until thoroughly combined. The mix tastes pretty good now, with the sugar and usually vanilla (or vanillin) blended in, but it's gritty. And texture—silky, luxurious texture—is almost as important to chocolate pleasure as flavor. So the batch goes into the refining apparatus. Here three, sometimes even five steel rollers rotate over the mass, smoothing the tiny particles of chocolate and sugar to about twenty microns each (a micron is one thousandth of a millimeter). Without this step the chocolate would feel unpleasant in the mouth, rough and grainy. As a matter of fact, refining still isn't enough for the best chocolate. For consummate texture, as Rodolphe Lindt discovered, you need conching.

In the conches, which are either rectangular troughs or, the newest type, round drums, the chocolate is stirred around again. The particles get even tinier and smoother, coated with the extra cocoa butter that is added now, often accompanied by the emulsifier lecithin. The movement and friction in the conches bring the chocolate's texture to utter suavity; the aeration harmonizes its flavor. All this takes up to seventy-two hours; less expensive brands shorten the step or skip it entirely.

Up to this point the chocolate has been kept fluid at temperatures up to 185 degrees Fahrenheit. Now it is cooled to about 84.2 degrees in the tempering, a process that prevents the cocoa butter from recrystallizing later and making the finished chocolate grainy again. For now, though, the freshly tempered chocolate is just the right consistency to flow through machines that will form the various confections that brighten our days.

Continental imports competed for the British market. Courtesy, Bensdorp B.V. Cacao-en Chocoladefabrieken, Holland

After 1900 Cadbury milk chocolate began to far outsell foreign brands in England, and continued to do so as the years passed and the label changed. *Courtesy, Cadbury Limited*

In the late 1800s machinery was primitive, perhaps, compared to modern high-tech marvels, but basically chocolate was manufactured the way it is today. And more and more of it was turned out as increasing industrialization made large-scale production feasible and increasing cocoa crops provided the wherewithal. Import duties, once so high that drinking chocolate had been the exclusive privilege of the rich, were lower now for the big shipments from new plantations in Latin America, Africa, even Asia. All the circumstances combined to feed the growing hunger for eating chocolate.

In the United States Maillard advertised in 1878 that its "celebrated Vanilla Chocolates" could be bought from "grocers everywhere." (Manufacturers trumpeted explicitly what later generations would take for granted: a touch of vanilla flavoring in their chocolate.) Shopkeepers stocked great slabs a foot wide, a foot and a half long, and two inches thick, from which they'd hammer off chunks that they sold for a penny a bagful, along with penny chocolate cigars. The government sent chocolate by the ton to soldiers fighting in the Philippines in 1898—not only as a treat but because, like drinking chocolate earlier, it was considered healthful, an energy builder. Many thought that it could take the place of all other food, that chocolate and a piece of bread made a completely nutritious meal. In Germany, a "Royal Prussian Patented Chocolate Product" upped the nourishment index by including a hefty infusion of meat extract. The amalgam didn't seem outlandish at the time; people were also swallowing "chocolate" concocted partly from the cocoa bean and largely from ground peas, lentils, or beans.

England's Queen Victoria sent *her* troops, facing the Boers in South Africa, half a million pounds of chocolate for Christmas 1899, and shortly afterward the Cadbury company donated a thousand pounds to a British Arctic expedition. The quantities were generous but not unreasonable. The English at home were eating thirty-odd tons a week of milk chocolate bars alone in 1902. Most of that was Swiss; only a ton came from the native Cadbury, which had added milk chocolate to its line in 1897, hoping to win away some of the import sales. Win it did, rising in a decade to outsell the Swiss bars many times over in England. Even before that, Cadbury had been prospering for years, and their Quaker social conscience moved the owning family to an admirable program passing some of their affluence along to employees. When they built a large factory for their expanding business in 1879, they offered high wages and shorter hours, paid vacations, pensions, and medical and dental benefits. By 1900 they'd turned 330 acres of their factory site at Bournville, near Birmingham, into a garden village where their workers could live, with attractive houses and careful environmental planning. A few years later they added such recreational facilities as a sports field and a women's swimming pool.

Chocolate seemed to inspire benevolence in its manufacturers. In Switzerland Philipp Suchard, too, gave his workers decent housing; he paid for their accident insurance, one of the first Swiss employers to do so; and was called "Father" Suchard in appreciation. But when it came to creating a paternalistic paradise around a chocolate factory, an American was the biggest daddy of them all.

Edward VII succeeded to the British throne in 1901, and the new king and queen were saluted in a rousing advertising poster. *Courtesy, Cadbury Limited*

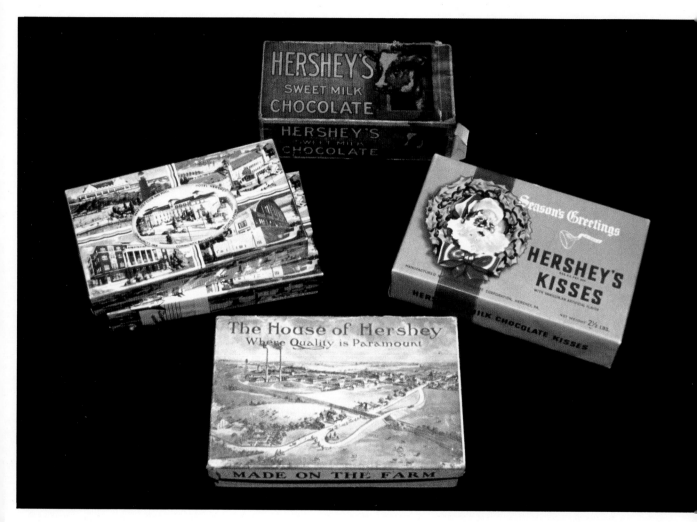

9

Hershey

hen Milton Hershey announced in 1893, "I'm going to make chocolate," the product was not entirely new to him. His caramel company did over a million dollars' worth of business a year—a noteworthy statistic in 1893—and two of his biggest items were chocolate-flavored and chocolate-dipped caramels. What was *new to him was the German machinery he saw at the Chicago Exposition. That year America's annual import of cocoa beans had risen in a decade from nine*

Old labels of early Hershey chocolates.

All photographs in this chapter courtesy Hershey Food Corp., Hershey, Pennsylvania

million to twenty-four million pounds. Clearly, Hershey was on to something when he decided that chocolate was a permanent thing.

He bought the demonstration machinery, roaster, grinders, mixers, molds, and all; had it shipped to his caramel factory in Lancaster, Pennsylvania; and hired experienced chocolate makers to run it and teach him. Now he was producing his own chocolate to coat and flavor his caramels, plus enough more to launch a Hershey's chocolate line in 1894. Baking chocolate was easy, but he wanted to produce milk chocolate, too, for eating. One summer he visited Swiss and German factories that made milk chocolate, but he didn't learn their recipes. Experimenting on his own, he set about using fresh milk, not powdered, because he thought it gave chocolate better flavor and keeping qualities. He figured out the right proportion of milk and how to condense it, how to add the sugar, what kinds of cocoa beans to blend, how high to roast them, how long to conch . . .

The resulting Hershey Bar was an instant success in the Pennsylvania towns where its inventor first sold it. So was its companion milk-chocolate almond bar, which soon followed. Hershey's new chocolate products were selling so well by 1900 that he decided to switch over completely. He sold the caramel company for a million dollars, a headline-making figure, and the new owners agreed to let him rent one wing of the factory for his chocolate. He had another product as well. Just as he who makes cocoa gets leftover cocoa butter, so he who extracts cocoa butter to mix into chocolate is left with cocoa. Presto—Hershey's Cocoa! Hershey promoted it simply. From New York he ordered an electric automobile, the first one ever seen in Lancaster. He paid two thousand dollars for it, but he got a lot of publicity mileage for his money. As the car rode around Pennsylvania, blazoned with Hershey's name, carrying his salesmen, it never failed to draw an excited crowd and a spate of orders. With his horseless carriage Hershey again made headlines. Despite its top speed of nine miles an hour, the newspapers reported, "The carriage is easily handled if the operator decides to keep cool."

The chocolate business outgrew its building wing, and that was when Hershey got his momentous idea. He would build a factory, but—and this was almost unheard of in America at the time—not in a town. In the country, the Pennsylvania Dutch countryside where he was born. In January 1903 he bought a thousand acres in a village called Derry Church. He needed space, because it wasn't just a factory he was building. Hershey was going to put up an entire town.

There were two parts to Hershey's great scheme. First, of course, the chocolate. He would manufacture it in such quantity that volume sales would make the Hershey Bar cheap enough for every man, woman, and child in the country. It was an early expression of the all-American idea of mass production, applied to chocolate. Then, the town. This was to be a pleasant home for Hershey's factory workers—if they wished. In no way should they feel compelled to live there. Even as Hershey supervised the installation of water and

sewage systems, he saw to the laying of trolley lines to nearby towns so that his workers could live elsewhere and commute to their jobs for a nickel. Similarly, residents of his town could ride the trolley to do their shopping in other places if they liked.

In the town itself the houses would be varied, individual, with none of the deadening sameness of the usual factory town. His employees could either buy or rent, whichever they preferred, at reasonable prices. There would be churches, schools, a post office, a fire department, an inn, a bank, stores—on tree-lined avenues named Chocolate and Cocoa, or Java, Caracas, Aruba, Grenada, Ceylon, Para, after places in the geography of cocoa growing. Hershey knew equally well what he did not want in his town. In residential neighborhoods, no "taverns, piggeries, glue, soap, candle, lamp-black factories, no blacksmith shops." Just outside town Hershey set an amusement park, a zoo, golf courses, a football field, a dance pavilion, an outdoor vaudeville theater. The crowning touch was the gorgeous (to use Roald Dahl's word) aroma of chocolate from the factory that was the heart of it all. When the town was renamed Hershey, it seemed only appropriate, like naming a child after its father.

Street signs in the town of Hershey today.

The factory a decade after it was built.

Milton S. Hershey with one of the pupils in his school.

The new chocolate works began production in 1905, "the most complete of their kind in the world," according to *Confectioners' Journal.* Almost immediately the milk chocolate Hershey Bar was everything its creator had hoped for: available everywhere for pennies, gobbled up by everyone to the point where no other chocolate, European or American, was any remotely serious competition. Hershey didn't even have to advertise. "Give them quality," he said. "That's the best kind of advertising in the world." The company followed his precepts, no ads, until 1968 when it began advertising in response to the pressure of competing brands.

In 1907 the line added Hershey's Kisses, milk chocolate tidbits wrapped in silver foil. (The little blue-and-white streamers didn't start twirling out of the foil until 1921.) The Kisses, too, were a quick success, even though they weren't a new idea. Since 1893 Wilbur, another Pennsylvania company, had been making Buds, similar in size and shape to Kisses and also wrapped in silver foil. But the Kisses joined the Bars in sweeping the country and earning Hershey a fortune. (Today the factory turns out up to twenty-five million Kisses a day.)

The town was completed, bustling with residents. In 1908 the mansion was ready, the splendid house Hershey built for his wife and himself on a rise just across a creek from the factory. He needed a new project, and he could afford almost any undertaking he could think of. He chose a patriarchal one.

Hershey and his wife, Catherine, were childless. They agreed that a satisfying way to spend part of their new wealth was to help needy orphaned boys. Hershey wasn't a Quaker, like the Cadburys, but his philanthropic bent more than equaled theirs. Possibly his Mennonite upbringing encouraged him to devote a tithe of his energy to good works on the grand scale his grand income permitted him. At any rate, in 1908 he and his wife donated 486 acres of nearby land and set up the Hershey Trust Company to endow a home and school for poor boys. There the youngsters learned farming and industrial trades with which they could later earn their living. Eventually the Milton Hershey School would occupy still more acreage and broaden its curriculum to include more academic subjects; its student body would grow to thirteen hundred boys *and* girls. In 1918, to ensure the institution's future, Hershey signed over corporate control of his chocolate company to the trust that administered the school.

Of course, for all practical purposes he remained in working control. It wasn't only that he *was* Hershey. He just doesn't seem to have been a sideline-sitting kind of man. In 1916 he decided that, with sugar so vital to chocolate manufacture, he'd forge closer ties to the ingredient. He acquired his own sugarcane fields in Cuba; he built his own sugar mills, and the railroad to make them accessible. Running true to form, he set a little workers' town around his first refinery. It was styled in the pretty Caribbean mode, with bright pastel houses and tropical flowers spilling onto wooden platform sidewalks. But it was fitted out, Hershey style, with schools and clinics, a golf course and a baseball diamond.

The factory in the early 1920s.

Then Hershey's attention swung back from his sugar town to his Stateside chocolate town. In the mid-twenties Mr. Goodbar, the renowned milk chocolate studded with peanuts, went into production at the factory, followed shortly by Hershey's Syrup of chocolate-soda fame, followed in 1930 by the Great Depression.

The town of Hershey had grown to include residents beyond the six thousand factory workers. But to patriarch Hershey they were all "his" people. He embarked on a building orgy that would keep them employed and, incidentally, would take advantage of the Depression's low construction costs. He built a high school and an office building. A community center enclosed two theaters, a library, a dining room and cafeteria, a photography workroom, a gym, swimming pool, bowling alley, fencing and boxing room, and a free junior college on the top floor. He put up the 170-room Hotel Hershey, borrowing sumptuous details from every hotel that had impressed him on vacation trips abroad. Then came a sports arena to hold over seven thousand for hockey games, a football stadium for sixteen thousand, four new golf courses, and the spectacular Hershey Gardens, which today are a twenty-three-acre manicured riot of roses, tulips, and an assortment of other flowers and greenery—120,000 plants in all. When the construction ended, the Depression was over and Hershey rested. "No man in Hershey was dropped by reason of the Depression," he said contentedly. "And no salaries were cut."

The town in the 1920s.

He died in 1945 at the age of eighty-eight, but his corporate heirs continued in his spirit. They added a convention center and a huge motor lodge to the town. The amusement park that had begun with a rowboat lake and band concerts turned into a kind of Disneyland with thriller rides in tune with the times. Today big fuzzy toy animals called "FurryTales" entertain children. They are, of course, people in costume, as are the larger-than-life-size Hershey Bars and Kisses walking around. A 330-foot silver Kissing Tower soars over the park, supporting a chocolate-colored observation deck with Kiss-shaped windows. Nearby, visitors ride in automated cars through the Chocolate World building, into simulated roasting ovens, on through all the other chocolate-making processes, and past living cocoa trees, which are among the very few ever to be grown successfully beyond the equator. (The Guittard wholesale chocolate company also grows cocoa trees, in the lobby of their offices outside San Francisco.)

The community of Hershey still smells like chocolate under the fragrance drifting over from the factory, but it's no toy town. With a population of eighteen thousand, it boasts an orchestra society, a string ensemble, a ballet school, championship tournaments at its golf courses, two award-winning public-broadcasting stations—one radio, one television—and the Milton S. Hershey Medical Center of Pennsylvania State University. Built with a $50 million donation from the Hershey Chocolate Corporation in 1963, the center includes a top-rank hospital, medical school, clinics, and research facilities.

The corporation that funded the center had been put back in control of chocolate operations in 1927. The business has since diversified into other products,

The factory today.

Kiss diameter is measured.

Kiss-shaped streetlights along
Chocolate Avenue.

98

A best-selling chocolate bar
being packed by the boxful.

and in 1968 changed its name to the Hershey Foods Corporation, of which the
largest division is the Chocolate Company. The Trust Company now only ad-
ministers the funds of the Milton Hershey School. Still another organization,
HERCO (Hershey Entertainment and Resort Company), manages the various
tourist attractions and many businesses in town. It adds up to an impressive
enterprise. The firm that began in one wing of a caramel factory is today on
Fortune magazine's list of the five hundred biggest companies in the United
States.

It's an American saga—this story of the Hershey company and its beneficent
fallout. And it was all powered by a best-selling chocolate bar.

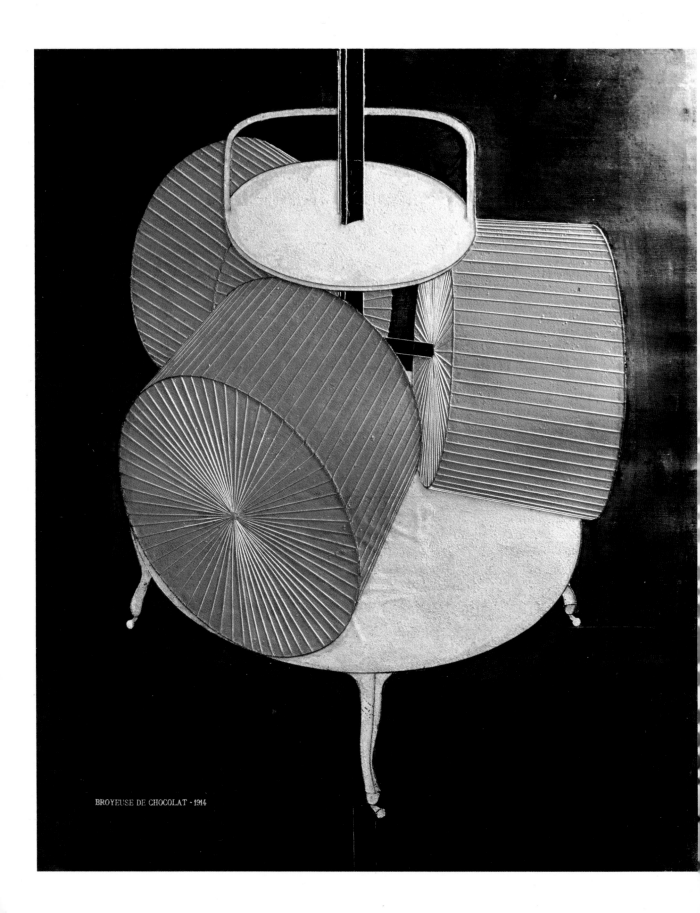

BROYEUSE DE CHOCOLAT · 1914

10

Making Candy

*B*ars are the most straightforward candy that
factories make out of chocolate, which we left
on page 81, conched and tempered, thick but
still rather liquid—just the right consistency
to proceed. Now it's transferred to a pouring machine
positioned above a continuously moving conveyor belt of
bar-size molds. The pourer shoots out a succession of
precisely timed chocolate jets to fill each mold. If nut or
raisin bars are being made, or flavored ones like coffee or
orange, the added component is mixed into the chocolate

Chocolate Grinder, No. 2 by Marcel Duchamp (1912), French. Best known
for his 1911 *Nude Descending a Staircase,* Duchamp also looked to human
artifacts for his subjects—as in this canvas, done in oil, thread, and pencil,
inspired by an old-fashioned chocolate grinder he watched, fascinated,
in a Rouen confectioner's shop window. Duchamp saw the kinetic mechanism
as an image for expressing the idea of action. *The Philadelphia Museum of
Art. Louise and Walter Arensberg Collection*

STEPS IN THE MANUFACTURE
OF CANDY

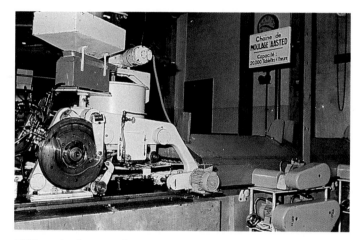

Filling the bar molds. *Courtesy, Société des Produits Nestlé S.A., Vevey, Switzerland*

Knocking out air bubbles. *Courtesy, Société des Produits Nestlé S.A., Vevey, Switzerland*

Leaving the cooling tunnel. *Courtesy, Société des Produits Nestlé S.A., Vevey, Switzerland*

pecting for imperfectly molded bars.
rtesy, Hershey Foods Corp.

Almonds set in place
inside a filled bar. *Copyright,
CHOCOSUISSE, Switzerland*

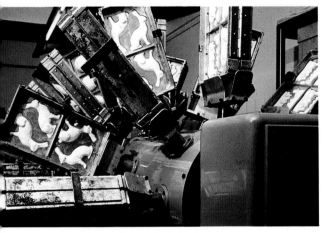

ocolate bunnies are made on a centrifugal machine.
yright, CHOCOSUISSE, Switzerland

Precut centers are enrobed. *Copyright,
CHOCOSUISSE, Switzerland*

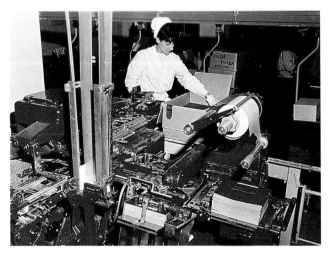

ling bonbon molds. *Courtesy, Société des
oduits Nestlé S.A., Vevey, Switzerland*

Packaging. *Courtesy, Société des Produits Nestlé S.A.,
Vevey, Switzerland*

just before it goes into the pourer. The filled molds move on to a vibrating machine that shakes them up to spread the chocolate evenly and get rid of any air bubbles. Then the molds, still on their conveyor belt, travel to a cooling tunnel where the chocolate hardens. The solid bars are shaken out of their molds and sent off to the packaging machines.

Chocolate bars can also be filled with fondant cream or a liquid—and often are in Europe, most particularly with liqueurs and fruit brandies. The Swiss say that Jules Séchaud of Montreux was the first to think of making filled bars, in 1913. The English point to their Fry company's Chocolate Cream filled bar, which appeared in the 1870s and, they say, "has a strong claim to being the first." (The Chocolate Cream is still on the market, under the Cadbury label since Cadbury's merger with Fry.) In any case, the procedure is similar to that for regular bars, except that the molds are a little deeper. After being filled they're inverted so that some chocolate runs out, leaving only a layer lining the molds. Then off to the cooling tunnel to harden; on to the next machine, which pours in the cream or liquid filling; back to the cooling tunnel. Finally, a thicker layer of chocolate is poured over the filling (this will be the bottom of the bar), and the bars return to the cooling tunnel for their last hardening before packaging.

Bonbons, the small candies that fill a box of assorted chocolates, were hand-dipped for a long time. In the late 1860s confectioners began to chocolate-coat a dollop of fondant cream, at first just as a way of giving the fondant a form so it could be picked up comfortably. It soon became clear that the chocolate coating was bringing in at least as many customers as the cream centers. Confectioners started dipping nuts, fruits, nougats, toffees into chocolate, and the public devoured them. Milton Hershey was so successful with his chocolate-covered caramels that, as we've seen, he was emboldened to go on to develop the Hershey Bar.

Hand-dipping became a minor art: knowing how to pick up the center and swirl it deftly in the fluid chocolate so that the coating was perfect, thick or thin as the dipper wished. But it was a slow process, not exactly compatible with mass production. About 1900 the enrober was invented in France, a machine that did the job faster and cheaper and brought down the price of bonbons. Enrobing is still the most economical—and thus the most popular—method of chocolate-coating. Cadbury enrobes many of its filled bars (some, the Chocolate Cream for one, are molded), but mainly the method is used for bonbons. Hard or chewy centers are precut and shaped in a separate machine, then sent via conveyor belt through the enrober to be showered with chocolate. Often the centers go through twice, to ensure an even coating. With better chocolates, the conveyor belt next takes them under nozzles that squiggle designs on them in varied patterns, sometimes in different colors of chocolate. Or the candies get a decorative bit of fruit or nut on top.

For decades the term *hand-dipped* indicated superior chocolates with thicker, smoother coatings; many people still think it does, and prefer the hand-dipped

Courtesy, Suchard-Tobler S.A., Switzerland

bonbons of some special, usually small, chocolatier. Actually, enrobers nowadays can control the coating as well as a human dipper can. And, as manufacturers are quick to point out, the machines are more hygienic than germ-carrying hands.

Liquid centers, too, can be enrobed. A mixture of hot sugar syrup and liqueur or fruit juice is poured into small depressions in starch-powder sheets laid out on a flat surface. After a day or two the sugar syrup separates out and hardens, encasing the liqueur or juice. The now rigid shapes are lifted from the starch sheets and sent off to the enrober for their coating.

Other chocolates—the more expensive ones, because the process is slower and more painstaking—are molded much the way filled bars are, only the molds are bonbon-size and prettily shaped as flowers, seashells, and the like. That makes the candies' top surfaces sculpted while the bottoms are, of course, flat. More ambitious still are chocolates that are sculpted on both sides. These are each made in two molds, the finished halves filled, the edges slightly heated, joined together, and cooled to harden. Chocolate figures—bunnies for Easter, Santas for Christmas—can also be made by joining together two molded halves, filled or not. Another method is the hinged one-piece mold of, say, bunnies. The molds are spun on a centrifuge to spread the chocolate inside them evenly and knock out air bubbles. The cooled figures can be left hollow or filled by injecting a fondant cream through a small opening, then closing it with a drop of liquid chocolate which hardens as it cools.

The twentieth century, then, brought innovations in the makeup of chocolate bars and bonbons. It also saw new national patterns in chocolate consumption. The Spanish, for so long the leaders, were outsnacked per capita in the early 1900s by the Germans, Americans, French, and British, in that order. During the next decade the list included the Swiss, who finally got around to appreciating the confection some of their compatriots made so well that they were winning gold medals at every international exposition. "Chocolate" was becoming synonymous with "Switzerland." In a famous 1908 operetta by the Viennese composer Oscar Straus, the hero, a Swiss mercenary, is called "The Chocolate Soldier" as a smiling reference to his nationality.

(In the field of dance, on the other hand, chocolate still meant Spain in one important instance. In the 1880s in Russia, the historic choreographer Marius Petipa had designed the *Nutcracker* ballet and Tchaikovsky had set it to music. The scenario personified various Christmastime goodies through dancers. It was explained a century later by the greatest choreographer of our own time, the late George Balanchine, whose *Nutcracker* for the New York City Ballet Company was a Christmas-season sugarplum for years—and still is, under his disciples. His Russian accent chiming through, Balanchine told a *New York Times* reporter in 1980, "Petipa made chocolate Spanish dance because Spanish came and found chocolate.")

One Swiss company, Tobler, came up with a European equivalent to the Hershey Bar; that is, a best-seller known to everyone. Toblerone today is sold in

"The Chocolate Soldier."
From the 1909 production of
the Oscar Straus operetta.

"Hot Chocolate" sequence
from *The Nutcracker* as
danced by Alexia Hess and
Peter Frame with the New
York City Ballet Company.
Photo by Costas

Courtesy, Suchard-Tobler S.A., Switzerland

107

The originals of Nos. 1. 2. + 3 were painted in the autumn of 1868. R.C.

No 1

The original was painted in the Spring of 1868.

Birmingham Gazette Nov. 8th 1869

CADBURY'S CHOCOLATE CREMES.—Among the pictorial novelties introduced to the trade this season, few, if any, excel the illustration on Messrs. Cadbury's four-ounce box of chocolate crèmes. It is chaste, yet simple, and consists of a blue-eyed maiden, some six summers old, neatly dressed in a muslin frock trimmed with lace, nursing a cat. It is designed and drawn by Mr. Richard Cadbury (a member of the firm), and reflects great credit upon him for its artistic excellence. The picture is got up in colours by Messrs. Goodall and Co., of London.—The Grocer.

No 3

Messrs. Cadbury Brothers, of Birmingham, have just introduced two new fancy boxes for their three-ounce size of chocolate crèmes. On one is a pretty marine view—a juvenile on the beach about to test the sailing properties of a fully-rigged toy ship; on the other, an exquisite picture of a mother and child. Both subjects have been designed by Mr. Richard Cadbury, and skilfully worked out by Messrs. Kronheim and Co.—The Grocer.

Birmingham Gazette 9 Nov 6. 69

Robertson's comedy, "Home," has been played to crowded houses in Birmingham during the present week. On the 22nd inst., in the opening scene, Colonel John White (Mr. Sothern) presented Bertie Thompson (Lucy Dorrison's lover) with a conciliatory gift in the shape of a box of Cadbury's Chocolate Crèmes. The dialogue that ensued was as much appreciated by the audience as the box was by the recipient.—

The box with the picture of Mother + child was the one presented by Mr Sothern + adopted by him through the whole of the kingdom. R.C.

No 2

No 4

The original was painted in the Spring of 1869. R.C.

No 5

The originals of No 4 + 5 were painted in the Spring of 1870.

over a hundred countries, including the United States. It was invented in 1908 when Theodor Tobler, son of the company's founder, was given the idea for it by his cousin, Emil Baumann. The two men, puttering in Tobler's kitchen one evening, combined his milk chocolate with honey and chopped almonds. They named their creation Toblerone, in honor of the chocolate and of torrone, the popular Italian confection made of honey and almonds. In honor of the Alpine peaks outside their window, they shaped Toblerone as a row of connected triangles. No doubt they had a practical consideration in mind as well; each little chocolate mountain was easily broken off into a bite-size piece. The whole conception was so unique—flavor, shape, and name—that Tobler and Baumann patented it, becoming the first ever to be granted a Swiss patent for a chocolate design. Today Toblerone comes in three varieties: the original milk chocolate, bittersweet, and white chocolate. They are by far the biggest worldwide sellers in Tobler's handsome line, and, supreme accolade, the 15.4-pound Toblerone has made *The Guinness Book of World Records* as the largest regularly produced chocolate bar on earth. All Swiss chocolate was selling well in the teens of this century, over thirty-seven million pounds abroad a year, nearly eighteen million pounds at home.

In Italy, in 1907, the Buitoni family, already famous for pasta, began making Perugina chocolates in the small town of Perugia. Of its many successful confections, one would become a great international favorite. *Baci*—the word means "kisses"—are wrapped in blue-starred silver foil, a mouthful of delicious chocolate around whole and chopped hazelnuts embedded in a smooth chocolate mousse filling. They have their origin in a love affair that Giovanni Buitoni was having in the 1930s with an older woman. The only way they could communicate with each other was via her homemade chocolates, each wrapped with a love message. Today Baci are still wrapped in individual messages of love translated into four languages to commemorate Giovanni Buitoni's unique love affair.

In England, Cadbury paired chocolate with the visual arts. Under the tutelage of a *confiseur* imported from France, the company began making fancy assorted chocolates during the 1880s. John Cadbury, the founder, had long since retired and turned the business over to his sons Richard and George. Richard, a talented amateur painter, inaugurated a series of beautiful boxes for Cadbury's beautiful new chocolates. They were the first boxes designed exclusively for the purpose, and some of them bore Richard Cadbury's own paintings. Through the 1890s and into the new century the boxes grew more opulent, made of plush and lined with silk or satin, meant to hold handkerchiefs or gloves after the chocolates were eaten. As the 1900s progressed, the plush wonders faded

Richard Cadbury's paintings—some, of his own children—which appeared on the first decorative boxes designed exclusively for chocolates. *Courtesy, Cadbury Limited*

Boxes of the late 1880s and 1890s, meant to hold gloves, handkerchiefs, and jewelry after the chocolates were eaten. Gold and red boxes were plush lined with satin or silk. *Courtesy, Cadbury Limited*

Art nouveau boxes, and one (*top*) hand-painted on a silk panel, from the first
years of the 1900s. *Courtesy, Cadbury Limited*

Illustration from a 1903 issue of *Femina,* a French women's magazine, showing guests at a masquerade ball in Paris. One lady is "The Star of the East," the other a popular cocoa brand. *Courtesy, Bensdorp B.V. Cacao-en Chocoladefabrieken, Holland*

from Cadbury's line, replaced by cardboard boxes. Extravagantly packaged bonbons would reappear in another time and place.

Cadbury meantime introduced its inexpensive "Milk Tray" in 1914, and it is still the most popular English boxed assortment. In the United States, Whitman did the same thing. After starting out as a Philadelphia candy shop in 1842, the company specialized in chocolate. In 1912 they launched their moderate-priced SAMPLER assortment, which went on to become the most familiar boxed chocolates in the country. The SAMPLER packages came with a chart showing exactly where to find each candy: the raspberry cream here, the nut center there. It was a boon to the bonbon pokers, and a stroke of commercial genius. Whitman imported their own cocoa beans and made their own chocolate; that was another distinction. A third was their distribution scheme. They

Courtesy, Suchard-Tobler S.A., Switzerland

Publicity ploy for a Dadaist age. *Courtesy of Bensdorp B.V. Cacao-en Chocoladefabrieken, Holland*

sold their SAMPLER packages, in ever increasing numbers, through drugstores—the old-fashioned kind, with soda fountains and the scent of vanilla ice cream in the air, and Whitman SAMPLER assortments on display.

Other American chocolates were different, being sold in the makers' own shops. Fanny Farmer, for instance, the nationwide chain of stores, was started in 1910. (They had nothing to do with Fannie Farmer, author of the cookbook and founder of the Boston Cooking School. The stores' name, with the spelling of "Fannie" changed slightly, was merely a tribute from their owner, Frank O'Connor, a candy maker who admired Fannie's accomplishments.) The slogan, "Made on the premises," referred only to the finished bonbons. Every town in America had at least one locally esteemed hand-dipper in the good old days, but the places were much too small to import cocoa beans and invest in chocolate-making machines the way Whitman did. Most candy makers, even big Fanny Farmer, melted down and dipped from the coating chocolate they bought in blocks from companies like Guittard on the West Coast and Nestlé in the East.

Nestlé had branched out beyond Switzerland. From the early 1900s on, its factory in Hudson, New York, produced chocolate for America according to Swiss recipes. What's more, Nestlé would go on to open factories in fifty other countries. Finally, it would diversify so that today it is the world's largest food business. Another Swiss firm, Suchard, inaugurated plants in Austria, France, and Spain between 1888 and 1909 and would expand to over a dozen countries, including the United States, as the years went by.

Chocolate making, which had started out in small workshops and simple water mills, became an industrialized affair of corporations, mergers, and international affiliates. Sprüngli bought out Lindt, the inventor of conching, for a staggering million and a half Swiss francs. Cailler, the first Swiss chocolate factory, merged with Nestlé in 1911; it would live on, keeping its own label, as the class act in Nestlé's line. Tobler would merge with Suchard in 1970 and continue on its own quality way, joined with Suchard under one corporate umbrella. In England the Fry company, first producer of eating chocolate, would merge with Cadbury in 1918; later Cadbury itself would establish a United States plant to manufacture its chocolate bars for the American market. In Holland the mammoth De Zaan company was founded in 1911; eleven years later it dropped chocolate manufacture in favor of concentrating on cocoa. In 1964 the American corporation W. R. Grace acquired complete ownership of De Zaan, but the management has remained Dutch until now.

This parade of activity was set in motion by humanity's sweet tooth. The more brutal juggernaut of world affairs would stop the parade dead a couple of times.

11

World War I to World War II

*I*n 1914 the industry's decades of expansion ended *with the outbreak of World War I. Swiss companies were hobbled by sudden export restrictions. War fever forced Milton Hershey in Pennsylvania to shelve his plans for building a community center and a luxury hotel in his namesake town. Chocolate itself was mobilized. Emergency rations, issued to American soldiers on patrol or outpost duty, included chocolate-sugar bars. The problem was that the men rarely saved the one-ounce bars for a crisis yet to*

World War I era, magazine illustration of Allied soldiers in France being served by a contemporary "Chocolate Girl" under a reproduction of the 1743 painting (see page 32).

Courtesy, Société des Produits Nestlé S.A., Vevey, Switzerland

come; they wolfed down the delicious ration immediately.

Some of the more tenderhearted doughboys did save their chocolate ration, or got hold of extra ones, and handed them out to starved local civilians. Ernest Hemingway, in his short story "A Way You'll Never Be," wrote about an American in uniform being sent ahead into Italian lines—Italy and the United States were allies in that war—as an encouraging harbinger that American troops were on their way. To prove that he's an American, "I should have a musette full of chocolate," the hero says. "These I should distribute with a kind word and a pat on the back."

Hemingway and James Joyce were the twentieth century's most important writers of English prose. In a crucial scene of the crucial English-language novel of our era, Joyce's *Ulysses,* the two parallel heroes—Stephen Dedalus and Leopold Bloom—meet for the only time in the story, and a cup of cocoa plays a key part. Joseph Campbell, a leading Joyce scholar, describes the scene: "Stephen's brief impulse of compassion for his mortified elder Bloom, and Bloom's

119

Western European chocolatiers designed posters in the appropriate alphabet for their exports to Russia. *Courtesy, Société des Produits Nestlé S.A., Vevey, Switzerland; Courtesy, Bensdorp B.V. Cacao-en Chocoladefabrieken, Holland*

reciprocally, for a tortured youth struck down by a soldier in the street, breaks the reign in both lives of the law of death, and each one gives to the other in the mutually sympathetic brief fellowship of the following two hours of the night (the only completely undefensive moment in the course of either's long day) the keys to the resolution of his impasse and the passage of the difficult threshold ... When knocked down, [Stephen] was rescued and taken in charge by Bloom, to be restored in Bloom's kitchen with a cup of cocoa...."

The scene itself, as Joyce wrote it:

> He poured into two teacups two level spoonfuls, four in all, of Epps's soluble cocoa and proceeded according to the directions for use printed on the label, to each adding after sufficient time for infusion the prescribed ingredients for diffusion in the manner and in the quantity prescribed.
>
> What superogatory marks of special hospitality did the host show his guest?
>
> Relinquishing his symposiarchal right to the moustache cup of imitation Crown Derby presented to him by his only daughter, Mil-

licent (Milly), he substituted a cup identical with that of his guest. . . .

Was the guest conscious of and did he acknowledge these marks of hospitality?

His attention was directed to them by his host jocosely and he accepted them seriously as they drank in jocoserious silence Epps's massproduct, the creature cocoa.

Ulysses is an intricate portrayal of middle-class Dublin life during a single day in 1904. Joyce worked on the novel from 1914 to 1921. When he made cocoa the ceremonial cup in a significant encounter, probably he was playing ironically off its utter everydayness by then. Cocoa had come a long way indeed from the exotic divine drink that dazzled royal courts.

Homey though cocoa had become, candy-counter familiar as the Hershey Bar was, chocolate was still fascinating in the 1920s. The Hershey factory in Pennsylvania had offered informal tours from the beginning. By 1915 enough people were dropping by to warrant a more organized Visitors' Bureau. In 1927

Delivery truck about 1925. *Courtesy, Suchard-Tobler S.A., Switzerland*

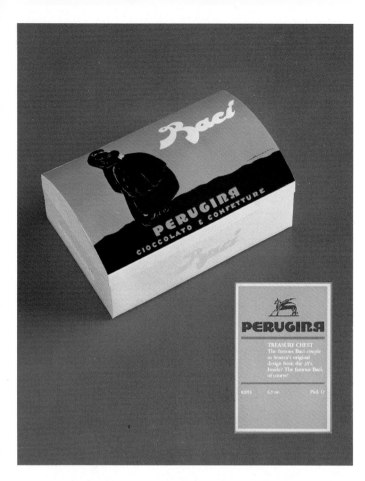

PERUGINA

TREASURE CHEST
The famous Baci couple
in Seneca's original
design from the 20's.
Inside? The famous Baci,
of course!

02953   6.5 oz.   Pkd. 12

PERUGINA

STROLLERS
Seneca's 1930's
impression of the
classical courtship
embarrassment: he's
brought chocolates for
her, she's brought them
for him. Perugina,
naturally!

02952   8 oz.   Pkd. 6

PERUGINA

HIGH SOCIETY
50 years have passed
since Seneca's elegant
lady hurried back to her
town house with a tin of
Perugina chocolates.
Times have changed but
our chocolates are more
in vogue than ever!

02951   8 oz.   Pkd. 6

PERUGINA

BELL HOP
A famous Seneca
advertising poster of the
30's is reproduced on this
handsome tin containing
a rich assortment of gaily
colored foil-wrapped
chocolates.

02950   8 oz.   Pkd. 6

Cadbury has long enjoyed the patronage of Britain's royal family, for whose members the company has named chocolate assortments throughout the century. The blue-and-white box in the foreground was dedicated to the present queen when she was a young princess. *Courtesy, Cadbury Limited*

The Italian painter Federico Seneca, who was associated with the celebrated Bauhaus artistic movement in Germany, created many award-winning posters for Perugina during the 1920s and 1930s. Among the most famous were these four, which have recently been adapted for modern Perugina boxes.

they started keeping count, and came up with a total of 10,673 sightseers a year. The annual figure would keep rising, to the million and a half who today tour the factory during one half of the year or, during the other half, ride through Chocolate World, the sleek exhibit the company opened in 1973. In England, out of its much smaller population as many as 100,000 bus tourists goggled through the Cadbury plant every year, until the company stopped the practice in 1970.

The twenties were the great age of the candy bar—the combination of chocolate and something else to produce everyman's treat for a nickel. Candy bars had first appeared in America in 1911, but they came out in droves during the next decade. In 1923 a Hershey employee named H. B. Reese established his own factory to make Reese's Peanut Butter Cups. The pairing of chocolate with peanut butter is today an American classic, copied by bonbon makers throughout the land. The original is still around, thriving under the same name, though the Reese family sold out to Hershey in 1963.

Reese's Cups have always been made with pure chocolate. Some other candy bars are not. Their supposed chocolate covering is actually a chemically concocted artificial chocolate, or compound chocolate substituting another vegetable fat for expensive cocoa butter. One candy bar, Mars, does use real chocolate; furthermore, thanks to its enormous international sales (even in Switzerland), the manufacturer is the world's largest single purchaser of the cocoa bean or its products.

With most candy bars and chocolate, the object has always been to make them taste as good as possible. One chocolate bar was different. The American Army's experience with all-too-delicious World War I chocolate had made it leery of emergency rations too irresistible to be kept, uneaten, to do their emergency duty. In 1934 Captain Paul P. Logan worked out the formula for a resistible high-energy chocolate ration that was called the Logan bar in his honor. It consisted of three bars, each four ounces, made of chocolate, sugar, powdered skim milk, cocoa butter, vanillin, oats, and added Vitamin B1. Maybe the oats did it—the new bar was an unseductive success. In 1938 it was renamed Ration D.

Three years later the United States entered World War II. The Army asked the Hershey company to develop a new chocolate ration, one that would sustain a soldier when he had nothing else to eat, and that he could carry in his pocket, unmelted, until he needed it. Hershey came up with a four-ounce bar, mostly chocolate but including other nourishing ingredients. At six hundred calories it provided a subsistence diet. It became the new Ration D. The Hershey factory turned out half a million bars a day as long as the conflict lasted. To eighty-five-year-old Milton Hershey's great pride, his company was given the Army–Navy E, a World War II award for civilian contributions to victory.

Chocolate was on everyone's lips during the war, not only as a military ration but on the home front as well. People were terrified that Germany or Japan would hurl a London-type blitz at America. Newspapers and magazines printed air-raid-shelter menus by home economists, suggesting no-fuss quick-energy meals. Almost always, chocolate was included. It might no longer be considered the universal food it once had been, but it was recommended as a peerless fortifier in battle and in siege.

That was chocolate's serious side. It also retained the lighter aspect it had radiated in the palaces of the French kings and the chocolate houses of London. No one remembered anymore its ancient reputation as an aphrodisiac, but in a polite way—1940 was not such a long time off from Victorian propriety, after all—chocolate kept tangling with the erotic, which now came prettily ribboned as the romantic. A young man went courting with a box of chocolates tucked under his arm. A red-velvet heartful of them was a Valentine's Day imperative.

Sometimes the old frankness peeked through. In the 1935 movie *Dinner at Eight,* Jean Harlow portrays a rich man's plaything wife. On the side she's carrying on with her impossibly suave doctor. As she waits in her boudoir lair for his very personal house call she is arrayed in all the accouterments of her sexuality: her froth of platinum hair, her vamp's bed jacket and beckoning pillows, and her glistening, greedy little Cupid's-bow mouth probing bonbons from the box lurking in her sheets. She gives new meaning to the word *sinful* as applied to chocolate.

Still more nakedly sexual was the World War II barter equation, the GI holding out a chocolate bar, the Fräulein nodding *ja.* Like the cocoa-bean currency of the Maya and Aztecs, the GI's PX chocolate became an all-purpose medium of exchange in wartime Europe. Mouth-watering bar in hand, the American soldier could go shopping for anything from antique silver for Mom back home to a beddable girl for himself that night.

It wasn't just chocolate, of course. Many Europeans had barely enough to eat, and people sold themselves or their possessions for treasures they remembered from the past, for coffee, cigarettes, sugar, butter. But somehow chocolate became a symbol of the crassness brought out by war's degradation.

12

Peace and the Sacher Torte War

*P*eace saw the return of chocolate's old nonsymbolic appeal. Once more it was simply a delight, and available. Swiss manufacturers geared up for high production again, freed from wartime rationing, export restrictions, and the relegation of overseas cocoa-bean shipment to a very low priority in the midst of global fighting. Cadbury in England resumed making boxed assortments, and Godiva started its luxury career in Belgium. Hershey in America went on expanding its already huge business, as

The Hotel Sacher in Vienna as it appears today. *Courtesy, Hotel Sacher, Vienna*

did De Zaan in Holland, getting a fresh start after the Nazi invaders were driven out. Perugina had flourished in prewar Italy, but then Allied bombing raids had demolished its factory. Now it began rapidly to rebuild and expand.

Soon chocolate was more popular than ever. During the 1930s, with a worldwide depression on, people had counted out their pennies for bread and meat, not chocolate. But the postwar period brought booming prosperity. Americans went on a consumerist binge, and Europeans followed close behind. Everyone bought cars, washing machines, snappy clothes—and chocolate as a regular habit, not just an occasional splurge.

Yet all was not well in chocolate land. Strife descended on its Viennese branch by way of a cake. Sacher torte had been invented in the city by Franz Sacher in 1832. His son Eduard, serving the cake at his elegant Hotel Sacher, had introduced it to foreign travelers and international fame. "I ate a lot of your glorious Sacher torte," Greta Garbo told reporters during her visit to Vienna in 1937. "To Hotel Chocolate Cake, Vienna," read the address on a telegram a couple of decades later, from an American who'd forgotten the name but not the chocolate specialty of the hotel where he'd left some important papers. His cable was delivered to the Sacher, of course.

You wouldn't think anyone could dispute the hotel's heirloom claim to Sacher torte. But Demel's pâtisserie boasts an eminence equal to Sacher's own. For two hundred years it has been pastry purveyor to Habsburgs and everyone else in Vienna who could afford it. Among its dozen superlative chocolate

The original world-famous Sacher torte. *Courtesy, Austrian National Tourist Office*

The interior of Demel's Pastry Shop in Vienna. *Courtesy, Austrian National Tourist Office*

In this turn-of-the-century advertising poster, the legend on the horse-drawn bus reads: "We eat only Demel's Chocolates." *Courtesy Demel's Pastry Shop, Vienna*

Sachertortenstreit auch im Patentamt
Angeblich allerletzte Entscheidung nach jahrelar gem Kampf / Hotel Sacher sieg te

"Sachertorte dispute also at Patent Office
Possibly final verdict after years of litigation"

Der Sachertortenprozeß ist entschieden
Die Konditorei Demel zog den kürzeren

"Sachertorte trial decided
Patisserie Demel has lost"

Oberster Gerichtshof
entschied Sacher Streit

"Supreme Court
decides Sachertorte dispute"

creations there was for decades an "original Sacher torte." This irritated the Hotel Sacher, and in the 1950s the situation erupted in a lawsuit that went all the way up to Austria's Supreme Court. Marcia Morton tells the story in her 1963 book, *The Art of Viennese Cooking:*

> For nine perfectly serious years, a battery of perfectly straight-faced lawyers argued the litigation between the Sacher and Demel's. The question: Which of them had the right to call its Sacher Torte the "original"? Crucial to the question—and here I quote from the perfectly serious court summons received by a star witness: "The subject of your interrogation is as follows: During the lifetime of Anna Sacher [Eduard's legendary widow, who ran the hotel from 1892 to 1930] was the Sacher torte sliced through the middle and filled with jam?" (The Hotel Sacher does slice and fill its Sacher Torte. Demel's does not.)

> Finally, on June 27, 1962, after the black-robed judges had soberly—not to say judiciously—tasted the rival Sacher tortes for the ultimate time, the fateful verdict came: The Sacher can claim to serve the "original"; Demel's cannot. This, despite Demel's position

The Café Sacher and the Sacher torte. *Courtesy, Hotel Sacher*

that the original was unsliced and unfilled and everything else represents decadence and decline. The judges, disagreeing, found that the extra layer of apricot jam represents, not degeneration, but progress. Demel's, bravely keeping its chin up, goes on serving its ineffable cakes, secure in the knowledge that it still is Vienna's leading patisserie.

Apricot jam—the placement thereof—was the bone of contention in Vienna's great torte war, but chocolate was at the heart of the matter. Sacher torte is beloved for the rich chocolate of its basic cake and the glossy, intense bittersweet frosting, which is poured over a thin apricot-jam glaze in Sacher's, Demel's, and every other authentic version. Thus, the Sacher–Demel verdict was sealed in chocolate. Sacher is permitted to set a round chocolate seal atop its torte; Demel must use a triangular one. A delicious peace has ensued for over twenty years.

13

Dollar-a-Pound Beans, Thirty-Dollar Bonbons

T he rest of the world is still struggling with its chocolate problem. Cocoa beans are the third largest international cash crop, after coffee and sugar, a total of a million and a half tons in 1984. The price has been decidedly unsteady over the years, going from three and a half cents a pound in 1939 to twenty-eight cents in 1947 to seventy in 1954, two dollars in 1975, and back down to one dollar in the early 1980s. (The average cocoa tree produces about twenty pods a year, which yield a total of about two

Courtesy, Lenôtre, Paris

Courtesy, Lenôtre, Paris

pounds of dried beans, the state in which they're priced and sold.)

The price depends partly on the ratio between world demand and a supply whose crop size is determined by weather and even by politics. Many cocoa-growing countries are politically unstable, and harvest management suffers during periods of turmoil. Ghana, for instance, was the leading cocoa producer for decades until the 1970s. After internal political upset it dropped to third place, behind the Ivory Coast, its better-run West African neighbor, and Brazil, first and second respectively now. Next come Nigeria, Cameroun, Malaysia, Ecuador, Colombia, the Dominican Republic, and Mexico. For the future, experts foresee a decline by West Africa—caused by, among other reasons, a shift in their economies from cocoa to oil, and a shrinking labor force as cocoa farmers move to city jobs. To compensate, a continued increase is expected in Brazil and, coming up fast, Malaysia.

Courtesy, Perugina Shoppes, Inc., New York

In many of the African producer nations the price structure is controlled by governmental Cocoa Boards, a setup that originated in colonial regimes and continues under independence. The boards generally buy up the national crop from individual farmers at a price decided by the government, and sell it on the world market at the going rate. These boards, plus other producer nations, and their customer countries have been trying for a couple of decades to work out trade agreements that would stabilize prices. They have not had much luck so far, since the top producer, the Ivory Coast, and the top customer, the United States (200,000 tons in 1983), cannot agree on a mutually satisfactory formula. So the price of the supply continues to fluctuate. As has the size of the demand in recent years.

More expensive cocoa beans mean costlier chocolate, and inflation plays a part as well. The once nickel Hershey Bar now fetches forty-five cents, a Swiss Tobler is a dollar and a half or more, and consumers walk away in that situation. In the trade they say that for every 100 percent price increase there's a 25

Courtesy, Bartons Bonbonnière®

Courtesy, Neuhaus (USA), Inc.

percent loss of sales. Demand did dip during the late 1970s, when cocoa beans hit two dollars a pound and the price of chocolate flew up in response. Disastrously, at the same time people worldwide were socked with a combined recession and inflation. But with the better economic conditions of the eighties, accompanied by cocoa's drop back to a dollar, consumption resumed its rise: up at least fourteen ounces per capita in the United States each year since 1980.

Price doesn't seem to slow the market for what are known as boutique, gourmet, premium, or luxury chocolates. Costing up to thirty-six dollars a pound (for Swiss truffles), they're produced by famous companies like Godiva and Neuhaus of Belgium, Lenôtre of France, Kron and a mushrooming number of smaller outfits all over America. The finest cocoa beans, the most assiduous conching, exquisite molding, and high-fashion packaging—and the price—lift these chocolates as far above the candy-counter item as a filet mignon is above a fast-food hamburger. Which is not to say that many taste buds don't honestly prefer the hamburger and the Hershey Bar. But on other grounds, what *Town & Country* magazine has dubbed "Choc Chic," people are shelling out for gilded boxes of chocolate jewels. For one thing, they make sensational gifts, draping prestige over the naked lust for chocolate. (Hershey itself taps into the luxury market with Golden Almond and Golden Pecan specialty bars, higher-priced, lusher-textured, and wrapped in gold paper.)

Of course, gourmet chocolates offer more than snobbism. Their fillings are satiny with fresh cream and butter, and no preservatives; though as a matter of fact, Hershey Bars, too, are made with fresh milk and no preservatives. But the finest chocolates boast a delicacy of flavor and a silky texture. The phrase "melting on the tongue" is the literal truth. Still, even within the genre there are snobberies. A representative of the French industry dismisses the chic Lenôtre company as "not basically a chocolate maker," and the revered Godiva and Neuhaus brands as "Factory-made! We would put them in the supermarket." In his own candy dish he would put only the creations of a certain tiny shop in Lyon and of another in Paris . . . maybe those of the Belgian Godiva.

For all Godivas are not equal, it seems. They used to be air-freighted from Belgium and are credited with awakening America's taste for luxury chocolate. In 1966 Campbell's Soup bought the American franchise. Today Godivas from the original Brussels factory are more highly considered than those made in Pennsylvania, though both cost about twenty dollars a pound. Aficionados extol the deeper, darker flavor of the Belgian chocolate, the largely hand-done sculpting. They rhapsodize over the more lavish packaging—handmade affairs of satin and brocade, velvet and feathers, reminiscent of Cadbury's turn-of-the-century beauties—while American Godivas come in merely stunning gold boxes. Motivated perhaps by sibling rivalry, in the early days the Stateside candies countered with deliveries around New York City in an eighteenth-century gilded coach. Really special orders were handled by a "Lady Godiva" in a body stocking, complete with white steed and minstrels, for a service charge of three thousand dollars. Regrettably, all that stopped. In 1974 the Belgian Godiva

Courtesy, Neuhaus (USA), Inc., New York

joined the American under Campbell's corporate umbrella. It's the way of the modern business-merging world. Italy's swanky Perugina (twenty dollars a pound) runs in corporate tandem with Buitoni pasta (under a dollar).

The abovementioned "deep" and "dark" are powerful one-uppers among chocolate cognoscenti, rather like the vintage-jockeying that goes on among wine lovers. Although milk chocolate accounts for 90 percent of American sales, and 75 percent even in gourmet France, a Continental classiness attaches to a preference for the dark. Proselytizers exhort us to leave childish things behind and graduate to bittersweet. The aristocratic tradition, they tell us, was

Courtesy, Neuhaus (USA), Inc., New York

Courtesy, Lindt Chocolate Products, Greenwich, Connecticut

rich in cream, butter, and cocoa, chary of sugar. Then, to prolong shelf life, cream and butter were cut; sugar, as a natural preservative, was poured in. Americans grew to love chocolate that was too sweet and too milky. Now, the crusaders congratulate, our taste is improving. More of us are beginning to want less sweetness in our chocolate; we, too, are looking for deep, dark intensity. Which leads us straight to the luxury chocolates. Oh, these provide milk chocolate for the unrepentant among us. But they pride themselves on their dark coatings, their centers made with pure cream and butter, and their restrained use of sugar that lets the taste of chocolate zing through.

Godiva and Neuhaus have their own boutiques. Perugina has one flagship boutique in New York City, and is sold at fine department stores throughout the United States. Other European luxury brands are available at select department stores: Belgium's superb Corné la Toison d'Or at Bloomingdale's in New York; Neuhaus at Saks Fifth Avenue, Macy's, Neiman-Marcus, and Marshall Field; Lenôtre, made by the *grande luxe* Parisian caterer of the same name, at various Sakowitz stores in Dallas and Houston and at Walt Disney World's Epcot Center in Florida. Kron, a New York premium firm, retails in three boutiques in the city and has branched out to Los Angeles and Miami. Los Angeles also has a dozen of its own gourmet chocolatiers; more and ever more American cities can boast of local masters.

American luxury shops don't make their own basic chocolate, any more than Russell Stover or Loft's does. For the most part the industry is divided into specialists: those who make candies and those who manufacture the "chocolate coatings" for them. There are exceptions. The Swiss companies—Nestlé, Suchard, Lindt, Tobler, Cailler—began as factories and continue, merged though they are, to make both chocolate and the confections they developed along the way. The same evolution explains why Cadbury and Perugina, Hershey and Ghirardelli, manufacture their candies from bean to packaging. The newer, smaller chocolatiers, even such luminaries as Godiva, Corné la Toison d'Or, and Kron, buy coatings from wholesale factories. Some of the best American bonbons are coated with Callebaut chocolate from Belgium, Lindt from Switzerland, or with Nestlé—milk chocolate Ultra and Broc, bittersweet Zenda, Newport, and Burgundy—made in America from Swiss formulas. Others use coatings from Guittard, Van Leer, Blommer, Ambrosia, Merckens, Wilbur—American companies whose names may be unfamiliar but whose products are tasted every day in chocolates ranging from Godiva to Fanny Farmer, from Kron to Candy Cupboard.

This doesn't mean that the scores of American candy makers have only a handful of coatings to choose from. A manufacturer like Callebaut or Van Leer blends a dozen or more kinds of cocoa beans into hundreds of different chocolates, many to the unique specifications of certain customers. Chocolates vary enough to elicit adjectives from floral to nutty, cheesy to smoky. Textures go from grainy to smooth. Candy makers can find exactly the coating they want at a price to suit their product.

The height of chocolate hip in the private sphere is ordering a ten-pound bar by mail from the manufacturer of your choice, for your personal savoring. Insiders insist that ten-pounders are on a professional level of taste and texture, finer than the life-sized chocolate bars of ordinary experience, and a wholesale bargain. The big ones certainly run a big gamut. Wholesalers usually offer several kinds each of bittersweet, semisweet, milk, and white chocolate. But you may not feel like taking a ten-pound plunge. All right, there's plenty of variety on the normal retail market, and price isn't the only guide. Even connoisseurs can't decide which premium brand is best, or whether any of them beats a good

Courtesy, Russell Stover Candies, Kansas City, Missouri

moderate-price bar or chocolate bonbon. (Fannie May, a midwestern brand, is often mentioned as a lusciously strong contender.) No one doubts the expense of making luxury pieces—the careful blending of centers, the beautiful molding or dipping of coatings, the delicate hand decoration. They just disagree about which chocolate they enjoy most. *Chacun à son goût,* it ends up.

Everyone to his own taste. And if his taste is for liquor in his bonbons, his greatest recourse is Europe. When it comes to chocolate, the United States hasn't yet repealed Prohibition. No more than .5 percent alcohol is federally legal in either imported or American-made candies. Three states have enacted legislation allowing more—Nevada, Kentucky, and Tennessee; in the last two bourbon-filled chocolates are a popular specialty. European gourmet chocolates, on the other hand, are often, and in every country, liquored up. Bonbons can be filled with Scotch, pear brandy, gin, kirsch ... you name it. Truffles are blended with Champagne, cream centers with Grand Marnier. Ireland has a chocolate bar, Wildwood, that's laced with whiskey. Such jollities can be brought in by travelers for their own amusement, but they can't be imported for sale in this country. They are truly in the luxury class, entailing a plane ticket if you want to buy them.

But alcohol-chocolate mixtures are available in every state in the union that licenses liquor stores and bars. In addition to the classic crème de cacao you can buy new hybrids, liqueurs flavored with chocolate plus mint, coconut, cherry, banana, orange, almond, or nougat. Bartenders serve brandy Alexanders (crème de cacao, brandy, and cream) and grasshoppers (white crème de cacao mixed with green crème de menthe). These tipples hold the only legitimate claim to the sobriquet "chocoholic."

14

The Chocoholic Era Meets the Fitness Epoch

Gourmet brands, though they gross over $50 million a year, amount to only a tiny fraction of American chocolate sales. Their buyers, on the whole, consider themselves connoisseurs. The rest of the over $10 billion annual retail product is consumed in good part by people who call themselves, with sheepish but happy grins, chocoholics. The word makes no linguistic sense. Chemically chocolate has nothing to do with alcohol. And the craving for chocolate, however acute, is not like the ravaging

© *1985 by Michael Skott*

dependence of the alcoholic. But when *chocoholic* was coined sometime in the late seventies, apparently it made emotional sense. It was taken up enthusiastically. The word seemed to express for thousands, maybe millions, their helpless feeling of thrall to an ingestible substance.

Chocoholics plus other more restrained American appreciators together eat about 10 pounds a year per capita. That puts the United States way ahead in total annual chocolate manufacture—well over two billion pounds a year—but quite low in individual consumption. Out in front, at 22 pounds a year per capita, are the Swiss, not surprisingly. *What do the chocolatiers buy, one half so precious as the stuff they sell* ... But the Swiss figure is probably a little deceptive. Cocoa executives say that it includes purchases by all those tourists who come to sight-see, to ski, and to load up on chocolate to take home. After Switzerland comes Norway, 16 pounds, though the Swedes across the border manage only 12.8; then Germany, 15.8 pounds; the United Kingdom, 14.5; Belgium, 13.9 (though the country leads the world in per capita consumption of bonbons, the art form in which its chocolatiers triumph; again, the figure probably includes tourist purchases—*if this is Belgium it must be Godiva*). Next, in downward progression, are Austria, Australia, the Netherlands, Denmark, France—and only then the United States, followed by Canada, New Zealand, Finland, Spain, Italy, Japan, and Brazil.

Consumer statistics are not available for the Soviet Union and the other East European countries. But it is known that they buy about 14 percent of the world cocoa crop; clearly they are devotees. China and Japan are converts to the Occidental indulgence. Both have chocolate factories, and the Japanese package their product with characteristically exquisite delicacy. Africans, with their hot climate, eat little chocolate. Or maybe it's just a matter of income—torrid weather notwithstanding, Saudi Arabia's consumption has almost equaled Europe's since oil made it rich. Many Latin Americans still prefer to drink their chocolate, but in Brazil the edible form has tripled in sales in eight years, sparked by two factors: the growth of native manufacturers to match the rising cocoa crop, and large European émigré communities in São Paulo and Rio, ready-made customers committed to chocolate since childhood.

Among all those happy nibblers, probably none believe anymore that chocolate will improve their health. On the contrary. In recent years fitness has become a universal credo, a grail, and a cause for worry, so that along with the pleasure of chocolate there was guilt—about what we were doing to our teeth, our complexions, our contours. Lately the chocolate companies have been spreading the reassuring new word from the laboratories. Chocolate does not cause acne, it appears; no food does. Under controlled experiments an indulger's skin sprouted no more spots than the abstainer's. As for teeth, it's sugar that makes cavities, and—oh, goody!—the harm done by the sugar in chocolate is practically *un*done by a more-than-kind element in chocolate that slows the destructive activity of the mouth enzyme leading to cavities. What's more, chocolate's cocoa butter eases the candy safely away from the teeth and down the throat before it can start trouble. Decay is much more likely with chewy, sticky bad guys like hard candies, caramels, and raisins, which hang around forever on the teeth, doing their dirty work at leisure. A much-cited Scottish study backed up all this, observing three thousand schoolchildren grouped according to the amount of chocolate they ate. The conclusion after many months: no relation between chocolate and cavities.

Now, about gaining weight. The chocolate companies are fond of charts showing the protein and vitamins packed into an ounce of their product, and its favorable calorie count (220 for a 1½-ounce milk chocolate bar) compared to other snack foods (230 for 1¾ ounces of potato chips). The companies do have a point when they mention nutrition: the cocoa bean is as natural a food as wheat germ, after all, and contributes a milligram here, a milligram there of minerals and such. Actually, it's the sugar in chocolate that bears the heaviest calorie load. Nevertheless, a chocolate bar is not a green-salad-hold-the-dressing, nor even a steak. Cram too much of it into yourself and eventually you'll be cramming yourself into your clothes. The best the companies can offer on the weight question is advice we already know: enjoy your chocolate in moderation, safety-cushioned by a generally balanced diet.

And then there is Katharine Hepburn. When it comes to chocolate, Hollywood's goddess of cool and slim is immoderate in the extreme, and says she is all the better for it. In recent years she's lived in New York, where she is recognized now and again in some little chocolate shop, on the trail of new delectabilities. At the age of seventy she was asked by a *Good Housekeeping* magazine writer to confide her secrets for still looking "terrific." Did she watch her diet carefully?

"What you see before you, my friend, is the result of a lifetime of chocolate," she answered. "A pound a day often." Thus outdoing the world-champion Swiss by easily a couple of hundred annual pounds. She added with a laugh, "Obviously, I don't have to watch my figure as I never had much of one to watch. Exercise, which I love, keeps me in shape."

As she and the writer chatted, freshly baked brownies scented her Manhattan town house, and she served him some from the platefuls scattered on tables and mantelpiece. Katharine Hepburn's brownies, made by her own elegant hands, are celebrated. A few months later she said of them in another magazine, the *Ladies' Home Journal,* "They are sensational. That's not very modest, but they *are.*"

Eat, enjoy, exercise, and you can be as slender as Katharine Hepburn. Unfortunately, some people can't do that, because chocolate causes uncomfortable reactions in them. They may develop headaches if they're sensitive to tyramine, which is found in chocolate (and also in red wine and cheese). People allergic to chocolate may start sneezing or feel queasy. But, contrary to the belief a couple of decades ago, doctors now think that allergy to chocolate is not common. For the unlucky few, health-food stores offer sweets made with carob powder. Ground from the pods of a Mediterranean evergreen, the carob tree, it's fondly supposed to taste like chocolate. Judgments on carob vary: (A) a satisfying substitute; (B) okay in its own way, but it does not taste like chocolate; (C) it's awful. It is, as they say, a matter of taste—your own, and that of the particular carob product you try. If your health demands it, carob is something to investigate. But don't expect it to be lower in calories or generally healthier than chocolate. It's neither. True, carob has less fat naturally than the cocoa bean, but balancing that is its higher sugar content. The finished confections come out equal: chocolate needs sugar to be palatable, and carob needs added fat, which usually is some vegetable oil more highly saturated and not nearly as appetizing as cocoa butter.

The French have another, almost ethnic health consideration—their livers. The Gallic preoccupation with the care and feeding of that organ is proverbial. (The American movie star Olivia De Havilland, who married a Parisian and lived in his city for years, wrote a book titled *Every Frenchman Has One,* about her countrymen-in-law. "One" referred to the liver.) So it was no small matter when a noted liver specialist, Dr. Bérand, wrote in his book, *The Frenchman's Liver:* "I am happy to be able to say to those who have more or less deprived themselves of chocolate over the years, that there is no medical basis to justify [this deprivation]." As a clincher, France's own screen Catherine, the radiant Deneuve, is known to like chocolate, and presumably her liver is as glorious as the rest of her.

A misconception about the effect of chocolate on the human body arises when people, learning that cocaine is made from the coca plant, think they're hearing "cocoa" plant. They aren't. The coca plant is an entirely separate botanical creature from the cocoa tree, and chocolate has no connection at all with cocaine. If the chocoholic is addicted, it's emotionally, not physically.

A less drastic concern relates to the presence of caffeine in chocolate. Presence, yes. Abundance, no. Compare the 9 milligrams of caffeine in a 1½-ounce milk chocolate bar to the 150 in a cup of strong coffee or the 65 in 12 ounces of some cola drinks. Not even the most frenzied chocoholic could gobble the amount of chocolate it would take (at least fifty bars at a sitting) to bring on coffee nerves. Caffeine, by the way, may be useful to the plants in which it appears—coffee, tea, cola, and cocoa. Scientists have begun to suspect that it is a natural insecticide, impairing the larvae and thus eventually killing off the bugs that feed on those plants.

Another stimulant is so endemic to chocolate that it was named theobromine, as in *Theobroma* (see page 27); it is extracted for use in certain drugs. But it stimulates muscles, not nerves, and is found in such small quantities in chocolate that it can't be said to have much effect of any kind when absorbed via a box of bonbons. Finally, if you have a blood-sugar problem, the only safe chocolate is the completely unsweetened type or the dietetic type made with sugar substitutes.

But chocolate isn't bad for most of us, and we can embrace yet another pleasure liberated from guilt. We can, in fact, rest assured that it's good for us.

Why, in the Alps, hotels tuck a chocolate bar for energy into every hiker's lunch packet, and what could be healthier than that? Sir Edmund Hillary, the supreme mountain walker, conquered Everest with a boost from chocolate. Going still higher, astronauts take it into space as a pick-me-up. And M.F.K. Fisher, the doyenne of American food writers, walking not on the moon but in the wintry hills of the French countryside, was heartened by chocolate. She tells about it in her 1937 book, *Serve It Forth:*

> "Here! Try some of this, young lady!" And he held out a piece of chocolate, pale brown with cold. I smiled and took it.... In my mouth the chocolate broke at first like gravel into many separate, disagreeable bits. I began to wonder if I could swallow them. Then they grew soft, and melted voluptuously into a warm stream down my throat.
>
> The little doctor came bustling up.... "Here! Wait, wait!" he cried. "Never eat chocolate without bread, young lady! Very bad for the interior, very bad...."
>
> And in two minutes my mouth was full of fresh bread, and melting chocolate, and as we sat gingerly, the three of us, on the frozen hill ... we peered shyly and silently at each other and smiled and chewed at one of the most satisfying things I have ever eaten.

And one of the most classic. As Mrs. Fisher certainly knew—she who knows everything important about food—French children snack on *pain au chocolat,* an oblong pocket of croissant dough stuffed with deep, dark chocolate paste. (American grown-ups have learned about *pain au chocolat* now that it's almost ubiquitous in some cities, sort of a chichi doughnut.) Spanish children in the Catalan southeast are given sandwiches of milk chocolate and the fragrant local bread. In Belgium *pâté à tartiner* is spread on bread. Italian, German, and Austrian *bambini* and *kinder* do the same with Nutella, a brand-name mixture of chocolate and ground hazelnuts, which is good enough to eat by the spoonful right out of the jar.

Such treats may indicate a lingering European notion that chocolate is a wonder food, in this case for rosy-cheeked children. In the United States, chocolate lately has been pleasure-coating a couple of foods worshipped today as the cure-all that chocolate itself once was. Granola and yogurt have appeared in American supermarkets in chocolate incarnations, double whammies for the chocoholic fitness freak.

15

Love and Other Passions

*I*t is amusing, when thinking back to the development of this {juvenile feeding} pattern in birds, to notice the extraordinary increase in mutual feeding that goes on in our own courtship phase. At no other time in our lives do we devote so much effort to popping tasty morsels into one another's mouths, or offering to one another boxes of chocolates."

The anthropologist Desmond Morris wrote that in The Naked Ape, *a study of human behavior. George Orwell dramatized the same idea in 1984, his horror*

Courtesy, Russell Stover Candies, Kansas City, Missouri

151

vision of the future. The characters Winston Smith and Julia live in a totalitarian society where chocolate is "dull-brown crumbly stuff that tasted . . . like the smoke of a rubbish fire" and sexual enjoyment is prohibited by the state. Julia gives Winston a piece of real chocolate, "dark and shiny . . . delightful," just before they defy the law by making love wholeheartedly.

M.F.K. Fisher mused on the subject in her 1949 book, *An Alphabet for Gourmets*. In all three cases chocolate came to the authors' minds in thinking about human love. "Gastronomy is and always has been connected with its sister art of love," Mrs. Fisher wrote.

> This . . . kind of passion that I speak of, romantic if ever any such brutal thing could be so deemed, is one of sex, of the come-and-go, the preening and the prancing, and the final triumph or defeat, of two people who know enough, subconsciously or not, to woo with food as well as flattery.
>
> The first time I remember recognizing the new weapon I was about eight, I think. There was a boy named Red, immortal on all my spiritual calendars, a tall, scoffing, sneering, dashing fellow perhaps six months older than I, a fellow of withdrawals, mockery, and pain. I mocked back at him, inadequately, filled with a curious tremor. . . .
>
> I was won, though, being but human and having, at eight as now, a belly below my heart. Red . . . slipped into my desk the first nickel candy bar I had ever seen. . . . It was a clumsy lump of very good chocolate and fondant, with a preserved cherry in the middle. . . . It was, to me, not only the ultimate expression of masculine devotion, but pure gastronomical delight. . . . My heart was full. I knew at last that I loved Red. I was his, to steal a phrase. We belonged together, a male and female who understood the gastronomical urge.

Mary Frances Kennedy, who grew up to become the wonderful M.F.K., was still linking love with chocolate in 1984, at the age of seventy-five. She told a magazine interviewer how her mother, young and lovelorn many decades before, had been advised by a doctor to eat chocolate to calm her pining. That long-ago physician was right on the mark. In the 1980s his seemingly fanciful prescription would be seconded by science.

Phenylethylamine, PEA for short, is a chemical found in the brains of happy people. Win a lottery, get a promotion, or fall in love—especially fall in love—and your PEA level shoots up. You're optimistic, sociable, peppy. But if bad things happen or if your love life goes wrong—especially if love goes wrong—you turn listless and depressed, since your brain's PEA is down.

Now, among foods chocolate is notably loaded with PEA, scientists have found. Also, they've observed that people disappointed in love tend to eat a lot of chocolate. The whole area of love and PEA is still under study, still speculative, but scientists are asking questions. Do the love-troubled eat chocolate be-

PERUGINA

HOLIDAY SPECIALS
A selection of imaginative containers chock-full of Perugina favorites.

SILVER TREE		
02081	5 1/4 oz. Baci	$ 10.00
CHRISTMAS STAR		
02077	7 oz. Gianduja	$ 15.00
HOLLY WREATH		
02078	8 oz. Chocolate covered cherries	$ 10.00
SILVER HEART		
03064	5 1/4 oz. Baci	$ 10.00

Courtesy, Perugina Shoppes, Inc., New York

cause they're instinctively trying to regain the PEA they've lost along with the beloved? Does falling in love raise one's PEA level? Vice versa, does a higher PEA level stimulate falling in love? And if the latter is true, does the PEA you eat get to your brain, so that every chocolate bar is a passport to romance? If this turns out to be the case, science will reinforce the eternal faith in chocolate as love potion—from Montezuma draining a golden goblet before entering his harem to Jean Harlow nibbling on bonbons, revving up for her paramour. To get at the truth, a stalwart band of researchers is tirelessly at work in the laboratories, "ingesting" (*sic*) chocolate by the pound and then testing themselves for reactions, aware that humanity awaits their findings. Strive well, ye worthies . . .

Meantime, one connection between chocolate and happiness seems to be established. Observing lab animals, scientists have concluded that certain cells of the hypothalamus portion of the brain send out pleasure signals in response to a substance either sweet or fatty. They go mad with joy when the substance is both sweet *and* fatty, chocolate being the most perfect exemplar of this. In other words, what we took for bliss is merely physiology.

Maybe so. But extramaterial virtues have been attributed to chocolate ever since the peoples of Central America centuries ago endowed their bitter brew with intimations of divinity. Europeans a little later on viewed chocolate as an almost magical elixir for health and well-being. Although Americans today enjoy an utterly delicious, caressing kind of chocolate, titillated taste buds and a gleeful hypothalamus seem too mechanistic an explanation for the cultlike fervor so many exhibit. They have their own magazines, with names like *Chocolate News* and *Chocolatier,* and in recent years they've evolved a tribal ritual called, variously, a Chocolate Festival, Chocolate Binge, Chocolate Freak-out . . . The names tell it all.

Chocolate has become such a passion, so widespread, that catering to it is lucrative for businesses beyond the trade proper. A hotel, say, wants a way to fill empty rooms in the off-season. It organizes a Chocolate Festival Weekend with a package rate for room, bath, and festival, as the renowned Fontainebleau Hilton of Miami Beach did in September 1984. The hotel's restaurant menus were dressed up for the occasion with extravagant chocolate desserts, bar cards with whimsical drinks based on chocolate liqueurs. The entire weekend cost ninety dollars. For three dollars the public was admitted to just the festival, set up in the huge Grand Ballroom. Five hundred companies around the country had been invited to rent sales booths; thirty did so. A well-known chocolate-cookbook author was hired to put on recipe demonstrations. A fingerpainting booth—chocolate syrup was the medium—produced abstract squiggles on paper and rapture in besmeared three-year-old artists. For adults a Chocolate Counselor asked the probing question, "Do you feel that at times your intense desire for chocolate controls you?" Multiple-choice answers ranged from "Every five minutes" to "Once a day"; a "No" choice was not provided. Hearing the replies, the counselor dispensed much approval and no censure. Responders

were sent out to browse carefree among booths selling chocolate in its infinite variety—candies, cookies, cakes, brownies, ice creams . . . There was one contest for best recipe in each of four categories: chocolate-chip cookie, ice cream, truffle, and mousse cake (a lush new genre, the rage coast to coast); and another for the champion ice-cream eater, with a ten-pound Hershey Bar as the prize.

The *pièce de résistance* was a "dunk tank," a vat filled with 350 gallons of chocolate syrup. Set four feet above it was a breakaway bench where celebrities sat in relays. Festival-goers paid three dollars for three chances to hurl softballs at the bench sitters, aiming to topple into the tank assorted local politicians, disk jockeys, and the stars of *Miami Vice,* a television series being filmed in town. The celebrities swam in chocolate, and the money went to a Miami children's clinic. Festival guests got a free (penitential?) exercise class as the weekend of indulgence ended.

The Fontainebleau Hilton had scheduled its festival hoping for two thousand visitors. They got five thousand, with lines forming outside the Grand

Ballroom each morning before the doors opened at ten-thirty. The management learned that weekend what Milton Hershey realized long ago—that chocolate does great business—and they quickly announced a second annual festival for the following September.

Grand prize in the Fontainebleau Hilton's recipe contest was a tribute to a forerunner, a weekend for two at Hershey's third annual Great American Chocolate Festival in, naturally, Hershey, Pennsylvania. This is the holiest of chocolate festivals, a five-day veneration that features more or less the usual events plus tours of Hershey's unique shrines: their test kitchens, the chocolate-scented town itself, and Chocolate World, the life-size mock-up of the cocoa bean's growth and manufacturing cycle. Visitors stay at the Hotel Hershey, seventy-five dollars a night for room, festival, and three meals, including chocolate-waffle-and-pancake breakfasts.

You'd expect a chocolate festival in Hershey. But Boston? The city sometimes known as Beantown, as in Boston baked beans, switches to the cocoa bean with Chocolate Walking Tours. Participants pay twenty-five dollars an hour for a shopping bag and the right to fill it—and taste—at shops around town, taking instruction in chocolate lore as they go. Festivals have been held in Buffalo, California, Chicago, Kansas City, New Orleans, New York, Seattle, and on a cruise ship to Alaska that somehow combined "seven days and nights of pure chocolate delight" with views of "the spectacular coast of Glacier Bay." No word yet of a French festival, but a group of chic *chocooliques* (they've Gallicized the word, which they find apt and engaging) have formed a Chocolate Munchers Club in Paris.

If a weekend of chocolate sounds rich, consider the international tours lasting from one to three weeks. Besides that Alaskan cruise, the Chocolate Lovers' Tour of Switzerland and another of Belgium have taken votaries into such hallowed precincts as Suchard and Lindt, Neuhaus and Corné de la Toison d'Or, to watch and taste. Others of the faithful have trekked through Scandinavia "In Search of the Chocolate Moose," possibly too hot on the trail to wince at the name. Israel, which had not been noted for this particular kind of pilgrimage up to then, in 1985 welcomed tourists to its week-long First International Chocolate Festival in Jerusalem. Highlights were the customary visits to native chocolate factories (Elite, which is exported to the United States, and Carmit, which is part of a kibbutz), recipe contests, exhibits, and a competition among Israeli chocolate sculptors.

Which brings up an ancillary branch of the prevailing chocomania. That people happily spend days, even weeks, and travel many miles to see chocolate, think chocolate, eat and breathe chocolate, is understandable on sensuous grounds. The stuff tastes so good and smells so terrific. But we begin to suspect that there really is something more to it than that—something totemic—when chocolate becomes a plastic substance to be shaped into icons of such national monuments as the Statue of Liberty and Calvin Klein.

Miss Liberty was sculpted by a chocolate maker in Barcelona, the city where

Columbus first reported to Ferdinand and Isabella that he had discovered America (but not that he'd spurned the cocoa bean). Mr. Klein, of designer-jeans fame, was done by an Australian psychiatrist who makes "chocolate photos" after hours. Other likenesses—either carved from a solid block or made from fluid chocolate poured into molds—have included Nancy Reagan, Henny Youngman, cartoon characters, the U.S. Supreme Court Building, the palace of Versailles, a Russian castle, a silver dollar, puppies, greeting cards, business cards, matchbooks, trains, automobiles, airplanes, boats, pizza, hamburger, petite marmite pot, decorative boxes, a calculator, computer and disks, typewriter, camera, cassette player, ski boots, tennis rackets, tennis balls, golf balls, baseballs, chess sets (in dark and white chocolate), Monopoly sets, rulers, alphabet letters, the word LOVE, and anyone you like sculpted or rendered in a "photo" by a mold made from a real photograph.

If chocolate is worked to look like many objects, in a reverse iconography many objects are made in the likeness of chocolate idols. A jigsaw puzzle is a mosaic of cardboard Hershey's Kisses. Kitchen magnets are bonbons or packaged Milk Duds, Nestlé's Crunch, Oreos. A chocolate-colored chocolate-scented Frisbee carries the Hershey Bar logo, and more Hershey Bars are slide rules, memo pads, and children's pencil cases. Erasers come as Mr. Goodbar or Reese's chocolate–peanut butter cups. Boxes for this or that are shaped like familiar chocolate candy bars or oversize bonbons complete with "paper" frill. For sophisticates among the cultists there are chocolate sundaes, parfaits, and mousses that are actually candles to dine by. And if by some cruel stroke of fate you're not allowed to eat chocolate, or not as much of it as you'd like, you can sniff it. An aerosol spray fills the air with essence of cocoa bean and your soul with comfort. Along the same lines, if your calorie regimen is down to subsistence level, with no leeway for even one chocolate chip, you can brew coffee beans or tea leaves steeped in "essential oil of chocolate" to sip in low-calorie sinlessness as you worship at the altar.

16

Looking Good

*P*redating the current swarm of things that look (or smell) like chocolate and chocolate that looks like things are the traditional artifacts: Christmastime Santas and Eastertime bunnies, chicks, and, of course, Easter eggs. Cadbury in England has been making chocolate Easter eggs for over a hundred years and now sells fifteen million of them around the world in a season. But the simple English foil-wrapped assembly-line product pales beside Italy's masterpieces—artworks that are created one by one, not in the millions.

These distinctive seashell shapes are a blend of white and dark chocolate and hazelnuts. *Courtesy, Chocolaterie Guylian NV*

In 1930 Cadbury still produced decorated chocolate Easter eggs. *Courtesy, Cadbury Limited*

Gorgeously hand-decorated, they can stand as high as two feet and cost up to a hundred dollars. Hollow bittersweet eggs are embroidered, for instance, with milk chocolate borders and traceries around a central motif of pink, white, and pale green flowers made of tinted sugar paste. Italians often order such eggs specially crafted with surprises like jewelry inside, as Easter gifts of double impact. Children get toy-enclosing eggs. Rodeo Drive, Beverly Hills' sybaritic shopping street, one recent Easter got four thousand eggs to sell—eighty dollars apiece, no gift inside—from the Pernigotti company. Perugina, Italy's best-known chocolate name internationally, exports many thousands of ornately packaged, inexpensive eggs to America for Easter. Perugina also produces eye-stoppers, modeled on the jeweled eggs Fabergé designed for Czar Alexander III in late-nineteenth-century Russia. The small solid chocolate eggs made by Peyrano don't match such visual *brio,* but they have their own quiet distinction; their nine different colors of foil wrapping indicate nine different chocolate flavors. Most magnificent of all, the De Coster company of Turin concocts a two-hundred-pound chocolate egg each Easter, leaves it partly open to reveal the spun-sugar tableau within, parades it through the streets to the acclaim of all, puts it on display through the spring, and proves that the seventeenth-century supremacy of Italy's *cioccolatieri* was no passing thing.

Chocolate needn't be an extravaganza to be impressive. NBC, the television network, felt that it looked good when for Christmas 1984 it sent major stars like Johnny Carson and David Letterman, not a case of Champagne or a set of gold-plated golf clubs, but a basketful of Hershey's Kisses crowned by a small pillow inscribed with the legend *NBC loves chocolate . . . and YOU!* Sensuous pleasure is the principal gift in such an offering. Along with it comes the sense of frivolous luxury that chocolate conveys, so that it's as socially elevated as caviar.

Chocolate can enter where more prosaic foods cannot. Take Park Avenue, the Manhattan boulevard where the wealthy dwell in aristocratic apartment buildings that stretch for more than a mile in a phalanx unbroken by anything so déclassé as a commercial store. For a few years there was a flower shop on one corner, but neighboring residents were unperturbed, flowers being so decorative. And maybe some appreciated the shop's handy sideline, a discreet trade in heroin. The sideline was discovered, the pretty shop closed by the authorities, and the premises rented by a new tenant—an enterprising Korean immigrant who thought an all-night delicatessen would be a nice convenience for the neighborhood.

The neighborhood disagreed. "Something is wrong in the universe," said one resident, watching renovations at the shop in the spring of 1984. "Someone has offended the gods."

Others formed a protest group against the "inappropriate" proposed delica-

A Christmas present for TV stars. *Courtesy, David Letterman*

tessen. They asked, "Do the residents of Park Avenue want to look out the window at *vegetables?*" And answered, "They most certainly do not."

The Korean entrepreneur scouted the city's fashionable food shops to see what sort of items might placate opponents whom he hoped to win as customers. He phoned one of them for her opinion, and she told him, "We do not want a food store of any kind. Flowers might be all right. Or chocolates. Yes, Swiss or Belgian chocolates."

The shopkeeper paid heed. When he opened for business, his windows displayed deluxe gift baskets. Inside the shop were a few vegetables—elegant ones like French asparagus and Belgian endive—plus flowers, caviar, French pâté and cheeses, over a dozen kinds of expensive coffee beans . . . And chocolate, lots and lots of chocolate. Fully a quarter of the shop space, up front, was given over to an array of imports. They were the first, mollifying sight to greet customers entering the store. As the shopkeeper told a *New York Times* reporter, his experience had taught him that good chocolate made good neighbors.

What is good chocolate? Chocosuisse, the trade association of Swiss chocolate companies, says it should have an "unblemished, silky sheen." When you break off a piece from a high-quality bar, "it breaks firmly and crisply, the edges are clean and the surfaces of the break do not crumble away. Your nose, too, can guide you in recognizing chocolate of quality; its aroma is full and rounded without being obtrusive. It smells of chocolate and not of cocoa. If you put the chocolate in your mouth the signs are even clearer; quality chocolate melts like butter. It neither clings stickily to the palate, feels gritty on the tongue, nor leaves any aftertaste. Its flavor is fine, delicate and unique."

"Bloom," otherwise such a lovely word, is bad in connection with chocolate. Bloom can occur when chocolate is exposed to heat or sunlight, causing the cocoa butter in it to melt a little and, back at room temperature, to harden again, producing a whitish film—bloom—on the chocolate. Bloom is bad for looks, ruining chocolate's characteristic glossiness, but it doesn't spoil either flavor or quality. Still, since good looks make food more enjoyable, it's just as well to avoid bloom by keeping chocolate away from heat or sun. A cool, dry place is what experts recommend, away from moisture; which is why Chocosuisse says that refrigerators can do chocolate more harm than good. If you feel you must refrigerate, keep the chocolate in its original wrapping or tightly sealed in plastic to protect its delicacy against the odors of other foods. Do the same for freezer storage. Chocolate does freeze well, but that recourse isn't usually necessary. Because cocoa butter doesn't tend to go rancid as other fats do, chocolate keeps beautifully—at least a year for the dark, six months or more for milk chocolate. With cream-filled, fruit, or nut bars, or bonbons with fresh cream or butter centers, it seems sensible to just eat them as soon as you can. Why buy ahead an item whose appeal depends on freshness?

Most countries regulate the composition of chocolate. In Switzerland the dark varieties must be at least 35 percent chocolate liquor, no more than 65 percent sugar; this would be "plain" or "sweet" dark chocolate. For bittersweet the proportions start at 50–50. Milk chocolate must contain at least 25 percent chocolate liquor, at least 14 percent milk, and no more than 55 percent sugar.

In the United States milk chocolate can contain as little as 10 or 15 percent chocolate liquor; semisweet is the same as Switzerland's sweet. The fat content of any chocolate labeled "real" or "genuine" must be all cocoa butter. Complete or even partial substitution by other vegetable fats, which are less expensive, makes the product "compound chocolate." "Artificial chocolate" is a potpourri of chemicals that are supposed to create a taste-alike, but no cocoa bean has so much as touched this substance. "Chocolate-flavored" products can claim a chocolate or cocoa ingredient, but not enough to meet minimum federal standards. In England chocolate can contain a 5 percent substitution of other fat for cocoa butter and still pass legal muster. In most cases the package labeling divulges the ingredient story.

The ingredient list for pure chocolate is brief, but the roster of its wondrous confections is long. Cookies, brownies, cakes, tortes. Chocolate egg cream, which contains neither egg nor cream, but chocolate definitely, in syrup form, plus seltzer and milk. Chocolate mousse, which does include egg and cream. Ganache, a kind of lighter mousse, made of chocolate and cream and generally used as a layer-cake filling. Truffles, chocolate mixed with cream and probably something else like Champagne or liqueur, to make a velvety rich morsel. Chocolate fudge, which the French explain to each other as "a very hard ganache." Bonbons, chocolate coating anything from puréed chestnuts to Grand Marnier. Chocolate soufflé and chocolate pudding. Chocolate ice cream, often flavored with cocoa powder, but in recent years a brand called Très Chocolat has been advertising eight "intense" variations all made with real chocolate liquor. Also, in a full-page ad in the *New York Times,* Schrafft's pointed out that it uses *"only* pure chocolate liquor."

Best of all, just chocolate. Milk or bittersweet, straight or blended with finely ground hazelnuts (in which case it's known as *gianduja*), flavored with orange, coffee or liqueur . . . Whatever your choice, as the man said, good chocolate makes good neighbors. Also good humor, good times, and a sense of pleasure in the world. Chocolate may not be the staff of life, but it surely is one of the necessary supports. Once the roof is over our heads and bread and meat are on the table, once we're freed to yearn for beauty and joy, for the extra boons that make life not a battle but a savoring—then we turn to chocolate as our just reward.

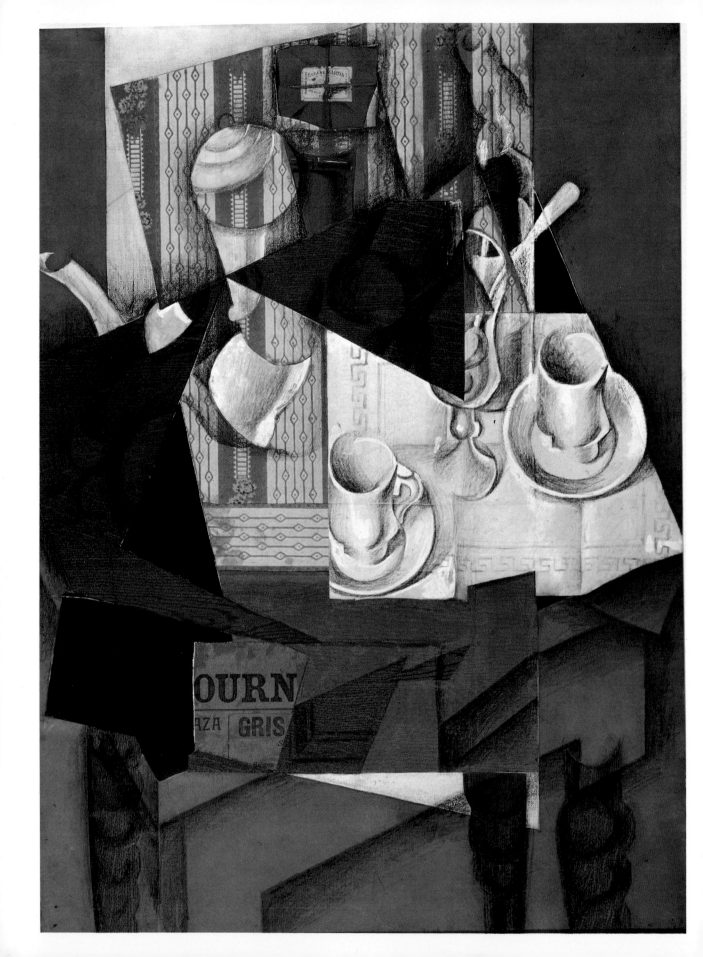

Epilogue

*I*n February 1985, a slim, attractive young couple named Delia and Mark Owens strode to the guest chairs on Johnny Carson's television show. They were there to talk about a book they'd just written—the story of their seven years in Africa's Kalahari Desert, studying the native lions and hyenas. For seven years the Owenses lived utterly isolated in those remote sands, with only each other for human company, with a stark minimum of water, meals of canned food brightened by an occasional ostrich-egg omelet, no

Breakfast by Juan Gris (1914), Spanish. Gris included the characteristically shaped chocolate cups and pot in this work—of pasted paper, crayon, and oil— and gave it the same title that Liotard (page 35) and Boucher (page 44) chose for their rather different visions of the theme in an earlier century. *Collection, The Museum of Modern Art, New York. Acquired through the Lillie P. Bliss Bequest*

television, no newspapers, no afternoons in the country or nights on the town, none of the amenities that normally furnish the landscape of modern Americans.

"And in all that time," Carson asked, fascinated, "what did you miss the most?"

Hardly missing a beat, Delia answered as Mark grinned in agreement, "Chocolate."

Even for heroic adventurers absorbed in their work, life without chocolate is life lacking something important. We take chocolate as a treat, a solace, a reward. Recently a manufacturer of mint-flavored chocolates ran TV commercials showing various people achieving various small triumphs: programming a computer, negotiating a garage-sale transaction, giving a music lesson. To cap each success the protagonist repeated the refrain, "I thank me very much," and popped a chocolate into a smiling mouth.

We reward ourselves with chocolate on good days and comfort ourselves with it after disappointments, or just revel in it for no reason except its own unique delight. The deliciousness of flavor, the lushness of texture fold themselves into every swing of our moods. To woo others, to flatter them or congratulate them, we give chocolate. Birthdays are happier, weekend hostesses jollier, job-promotees more jubilant, when a gift of chocolate celebrates the occasion. And what would Valentine's Day or Mother's Day be without it?

You don't need to be hungry to crave chocolate. A good meal can invite the final note of chocolate's luxuriance on the tongue, its fragrant resonance in the mouth. But if you *are* hungry, a morsel, rich and tasty, will feed you and pleasure you while you wait for more serious nourishment. Because it tastes so incomparably good, chocolate is pure fun. To paraphrase Brillat-Savarin: it delights us at lunch, cheers us in the afternoon, and enchants us after dinner.

Next time you take up a piece, aromatic and glossy, and raise it to your lips, and sigh a little in anticipation . . . stop for a moment and murmur a word of thanks to our immortal benefactor, Quetzalcoatl.

Index